WHAT REALLY MATTERS

Also by Eugenia Price

FICTION

St. Simons Trilogy

Lighthouse
New Moon Rising
The Beloved Invader

Florida Trilogy

Don Juan McQueen
Maria
Margaret's Story

Savannah Quartet

Savannah
To See Your Face Again
Before the Darkness Falls
Stranger in Savannah

Georgia Trilogy

Bright Captivity

NONFICTION

Discoveries
The Burden Is Light
Early Will I Seek Thee
Share My Pleasant Stones
Woman to Woman
What Is God Like?
Beloved World
A Woman's Choice
God Speaks to Women Today
The Wider Place
Make Love Your Aim
Just as I Am

Learning to Live from the Gospels
The Unique World of Women
Learning to Live from the Acts
St. Simons Memoir
Leave Yourself Alone
Diary of a Novel
No Pat Answers
Getting Through the Night
What Really Matters
Another Day
At Home on St. Simons

WHAT REALLY MATTERS

*What Is Truly Essential to
the Authentic Christian Life*

Eugenia Price

TURNER

PUBLISHING COMPANY

Turner Publishing Company

Nashville, Tennessee

www.turnerpublishing.com

What Really Matters

Cover design: Bruce Gore

Library of Congress Cataloging-in-Publication Data Upon Request

9781684427482   Paperback
9781684427499   Hardback
9781684427505   eBook

Printed in the United States of America

17 18 19 20 10 9 8 7 6 5 4 3 2 1

For Reba Spann

PREFACE

When this book is published, I will have lived thirty-three years as a follower of Jesus Christ—half my life. This significant point on my earthly journey seemed an appropriate time to set down some of what has come to matter most to me as a Christian.

It is important that both reader and author share an understanding of what is meant in these pages by the question posed in the title: *What really matters?* When that phrase is used in conversation, we generally mean to emphasize an idea or concept as being essential. We say: Faith really matters. Or prayer really matters. Or giving really matters; growth, service, praise, and commitment really matter. They do, along with what we are like, what God is like, and so on. Each of these does matter.

But as I see it, only the final chapter is *central*. The final chapter—His *commitment* to us—is central because once God's commitment to us becomes a part of our consciousness, *everything* from *faith* to giving happens as a result.

There is, then, no further need to attempt to whip up faith or generosity or service or growth or praise or any other characteristic of the Christian life. Realization of the content of the final chapter eliminates the necessity for futile self-effort. If God's eternal commitment to us has become reality there is no longer even the temptation to flaunt our own "spirituality" or shout our "victories" from the housetops. The Christian life that depends on His consistent involvement does not collapse in the face of trouble or failure or tragedy–if we focus on the fact that God meant it when He said that He would *never* leave us or forsake us. The content of all these chapters makes up the whole and none should be compartmentalized or sought after for its own sake. Faith, for example, becomes natural when we know something of the real nature of the God who has committed Himself to us. Without that knowledge, to seek, however earnestly, for faith, for a meaningful prayer life, for a charitable heart, for any of the other Christian traits, can throw us off balance.

From the moment of my initial turning one fact has been central: *Since God came in Jesus Christ to live among us as One with the Father, no one ever again need be confused about the nature of the Creator God.*

At the moment of my conversion that fact was central. Thirty-three years later it is still central. Counting on the *fact* of His nature and of His commitment to us all is, as I see it, the Christian's first priority. Accepting this *fact* relieves us of so much self-concern. It sharpens our sense of humor and adds to our courage.

None of this, of course, is original thinking. The Apostle Paul said it succinctly: "To me to live is Christ."

By that central truth alone I am able to keep my balance.

The content of each chapter is important, but if we try to place any single one in the center, our lives will tip to one side, throwing us off balance. Only He is the eternal weight of glory. With Him at the center we don't tip. It is Jesus Christ Himself who really matters—and because of His nature. He is eternally committed to each one of us.

EUGENIA PRICE
St. Simons Island, Georgia
March 1982

WHAT
REALLY
MATTERS

1

IS IT FAITH?

I had not been inside a church for eighteen years at the time of my conversion to Christ. My mother had seen to the "baptism and dedication of her firstborn" I had attended Sunday School and, under duress, church services, until I was free to go to a university and make my own choices. So, at thirty-three, I had no background of personal *conscious* faith or Biblical understanding to guide me after my personal encounter with Christ in 1949. Through the years those of certain religious persuasions have argued: "But faith was there in your subconscious." Perhaps it was. But at the light-shot moment in a hotel room in New York while my patient, sensitive friend Ellen Riley Urquhart waited—so far as I knew, I made my own first leap of faith.

I did not put my faith in the Bible—I knew it only as fine English literature. I did not put my faith in any church; I hadn't been near one—except that morning to please Ellen—in eighteen years. I did not put my faith in anyone's explanation of salvation. I did not put my faith in anything resem bling a heavenly reward. Oh, the relief was enormous when I understood that I would not someday just be snuffed out, made extinct at physical death, but that realization didn't motivate me then. Nor did I put my faith in the notion that God could now begin "to use my talent."

On October 2, 1949, my faith moved—because my attention moved to the Person of Jesus Christ.

The story of my conversion is told in a book I wrote called *The Burden Is Light*. What still stands so clearly in my mem ory is the invasion of my mind at that moment—and, of course, of my heart—by the Man God Himself. Through Him I could find out, as the years went by, what God's intentions really are toward the entire human race.

My faith—and indeed it is true that we do "have access to Him because of our faith"—enabled me to make that leap, small and untried and weak as that faith must have been. But I did not leap toward any fruit of the life in Christ. I didn't know about fruits then. My faith leaped toward God Himself because my friend assured me that Jesus knew what He was talking about when He declared: "I and the Father are one."

She didn't quote that Scripture to me. That was one thing I had forbidden her to do—fling texts. The Bible now is essen- tial to my continuing understanding of the "Life hid with Christ." Then, because of my prickles and rebellions, which God knew and understood far more clearly than I, He had to do it all Himself. And, of course. He was perfectly able to do that. Oh, if you've read *The Burden Is Light*, you know I read at random in the Old Testament the night before my conversion, and I admit that the reading created a terrible home-sickness in me. But at the moment when faith was born to my conscious mind I was convinced of one truth and one only: The young Man hanging on His cross was all that could be contained of the Almighty God in human form. And by knowing Him, I could know God.

He was central then. He is central now.

That first moment of conscious faith must exist. Where does it come from? Did I whip it up that long-ago Sunday afternoon in New York? Did my friend have such articulate and persuasive powers of speech that she talked me into it? No.

My faith, as did yours if you have faith in Jesus Christ, came from Him. Have you noticed that I used the word "moved" in connection with my initial faith? I *moved* toward Him because there moved into my consciousness the firm conviction that indeed, God would be discoverable to me if I dared to get acquainted with Jesus Christ.

Of course, words are always inadequate to describe anything related to *faith*. But after all these years I still remember a sense of movement, of invasion. He Himself gave me that faith at the moment my heart opened. Only He knows when a heart is open. He knew with you. He knows right now with you. He knew with me and He supplied the faith.

My sense of wonder when much later I found Hebrews 12:2—"Jesus, the author and finisher of our faith..." was dazzling. I thought, of course! I can understand about authors. An author begins a book and the same author is still there for the last page. I couldn't put it out of my mind: *He* began my faith Himself. It wasn't my doing, it was His. "Jesus, the author and finisher of our faith." As year follows year this divine Author, because of our encounter that day so long ago, has kept right at it—the way authors have to keep at it, day in and day out, strengthening, editing, refining the faith He began.

All of which brings us to what is often one of the most ridiculous points of confusion with Christians: a sense of comparison where faith is concerned.

Only last night I told one of my dearest friends about the recent awesome working of God in my life in regard to my profession. I was—still am—in awe of His timing. Carefully, as though I were a child, He had guided me by one seemingly insignificant event or fragment of conversation to another, until a desperately needed end was reached. My need had been desperate. Through the ordeal He saw to it—only because I *finally* stopped to listen—that I did not become desperate. And, following His careful guidance, I made a decision I should have made long ago. One I undoubtedly would have made ten years ago had I not been too "busy" to listen.

When I finished my story, this friend—a strong, childlike Christian—said: "That's marvelous!" Then she thought a minute. "But your faith is so much stronger than most people's faith."

I love my friend and so I just looked at her, searching for the right words. "You know," I said at last, "that is very hard for me to take. It's so beside the point, I really don't know what to say."

What was I *trying* to say to her?

Perhaps something like this: In the first place, for once my need had arisen through no fault of my own. And because it wasn't due to anything I'd done or not done, I didn't feel any necessity to repent and so I just stewed and fidgeted and tried over and over again to find a way to get myself out of the problem. And *only* when I found that I couldn't do one single thing did I turn to God with an open, helpless heart. My faith didn't seem strong at all. Oh, the problem had not altered my basic faith in Christ. That held. Nothing had changed Him. But I made no conscious attempt whatsoever to turn my problem over to Him. Don't I know better? Of course I do. But my attention was on my problem.

At long last He managed—this divine Author—to get me quiet enough to listen. To permit Him to bring to my memory a particularly strong reassurance He'd given me six months earlier, as I was reading in the Book of Job, before I even knew the problem was coming. What I felt He had meant then was to show me that I had been, for several years, running my own professional life my way. Oh, I stay in touch with Him all day long as I work-in my thoughts.

They are not high-flown, spiritual thoughts, rather inner cries for help with a stubborn paragraph, my aching back, the pressure of time, and so on. Yet, six months earlier, as I sat reading the superb literature of Job, a sense of God's power-a sense of the sufficiency of that power to ease the burden for anyone-had come to me. I hadn't forgotten that-except when I was flailing about trying to exert my own puny power. I came to the end of myself and of course, He was there, with all the renewed faith I needed to begin to work my way out of the problem. This book came to me during that interim, as well as another small book on handling grief. *Getting Through the Night.* He not only supplied the renewed faith to work my way through the problem, He made something creative out of it. I've never worked harder, and yet I feel as though I've been a delighted bystander. Most important. He taught me, by allowing the problem to drive home its own lesson, that I had been "playing God" in my own life.

And so, when my friend spoke as she did about my enor
mous faith, I was flabbergasted. I didn't know how to answer her adequately.

Of course, when I tried, the thought of the mustard seed
flashed through my mind, and she said, "Yes, I know, *but*—"
Well, Jesus Himself brought up that mustard seed. It is one
of His most striking metaphors. Was Jesus, when He told
His disciples that they could move mountains if their faith
were like a mustard seed, referring to the size of the tiny
seed? Un doubtedly, but I find the light I need to grasp the
metaphor in the Amplified Version:

> For truly, if you have faith (*that is living*) like a grain
> of mustard seed, you can say to this mountain. Move
> from here to yonder place and it will move, and noth-
> ing shall be impossible to you.

The italics are mine, but the amplification "*that is living*"
holds the secret. An occasional newer translation uses the
word "little"—"faith as *little* as a mustard seed." I believe
Jesus was referring to size in order to emphasize that the
so-called size of our faith is not what matters. The *quality*
matters. The "living" quality of a faith the size of a mustard
seed.

I don't really think I know what "great faith" means. We
all have faith in our esophagus—or we'd never dare eat a
bite. Once we've swallowed, from that point it's all up to organs over which we have no conscious control. Organs such
as our esophagus, stomach, and intestines, whose walls are
made up of involuntary muscles. We have faith in airplane
pilots and surgeons—even dentists. At least, we submit.

Isn't the *quality* of our faith in God the secret? And isn't your faith in any process or any person—from digestion to the pilot flying your plane—formed according to both need and confidence? In the old days I loved to fly. I still like the actual flight, in spite of what one endures on the ground waiting. But once I flew across the country with a pilot whom I *knew*, not only personally, but by reputation. We flew through three dangerous storms and I didn't even grow anxious. I knew *who* was flying the plane.

Is all faith in God a "given," as mine seemed to be? Does God give faith to everyone who has it? Yes. And that is as far as I can go in explaining that all-important initial leap of faith. *He* is the Author. But He is also the magnet. There are times when I feel almost as though I had no choice. We do have. We choose whether to take the plunge or not. And it isn't always a "plunge," either. Some faith slips slowly and quietly into being the way spring comes. Its source is God Himself wooing us to Him, and sometimes this takes months or years. Not everyone has a sudden conversion. Paul did, but I've read nothing about Peter's conversion, or John's. They simply got to know Jesus, listened to Him, talked with Him, opened their hearts and minds to Him. Then they were drawn to Him, so that when He said, "Follow me," they did. ". . . if I be lifted up I will draw all men unto me."

If He is even glimpsed *as He is*—not as priests, ministers and scholars have often imagined Him to be, according to this or that doctrine—He *does draw*. That is why it *seemed* as though I had no choice, once I came to see that God had paid a visit to us in order to reveal Himself in Jesus.

Almost everyone is familiar with the last three verses in the eleventh chapter of the Gospel of Matthew:

Come unto me, all ye that labour and are heavy lad-
en, and I will give you rest. Take my yoke upon you,
and *learn of me*; for I am meek and lowly in heart:
and ye shall find rest unto your souls. For my yoke is
easy, and my burden is light.

Almost everyone is familiar with that passage, but it is
the rest or the shared yoke or the lightened burden which
gets our attention. The key to all three certainly is in that
one phrase italicized above: *learn of me*.

"Learn of me, find out what I'm really like." As surely as
He took the time and trouble to hold out His scarred hands
to Thomas in order to calm the disciple's doubts, Jesus is
saying to us now that if we wall concentrate on Him, study
every truth we can find about Him, converse with Him, listen to Him, attempt to follow Him, faith is the last thing
with which any of us needs to struggle.

The following analogy appears in one form or another
throughout my work of the past quarter century and it is
now more vital, clearer, to me than ever before. When I was
in college, I overdid the typical student's requests for money
from home. But when Mother told me on long distance (I
had called collect, of course) that she would "get it in the
mail tomorrow," I simply waited for the money to come.

I had faith that she was telling me the truth. I knew her to
be dependable. *I knew my mother.* I did not stay awake that
night tossing and turning, trying to whip up faith in her—I
knew her. She gave me birth, cared for me when I could not
care for myself. She loved me. I said good-bye, hung up the
telephone all those times, went to bed, and simply went to
sleep *knowing* that my money would be there on the dormi
tory mail table the day after tomorrow.

When a trusted friend agrees to meet you at a certain restaurant for luncheon on Wednesday, do you spend the time until then attempting to capture a feeling that you can recognize as faith that he or she won't break the promise? No. You simply dress, get in your car or on a bus, and go. *You know your friend.*

If an author is known, if a publisher knows the author's past sales record, something of the loyalty of the author's readers, has confidence that the author is professional enough to do all in his or her power to deliver the manuscript on time, the publisher with a fair amount of confidence advances the author money to live on, and then waits. When he knows the book is at least half finished, he sets a publication date—as definite as is possible in any business—upon which you, the reading public, will be able to buy the finished book. Reasonable confidence, this is called. But it is also a particular kind of faith and it is predicated mainly upon how well the author is *known*.

The Author of our faith gave us one simple direction which, as I see it now, brings to us almost automatic faith. He does not wave a magic wand. He says: "Learn of me." Find Me out. Discover My true nature. Discover My deep-down heart-intentions toward you and every other person in My world. Does that make it all too general that He loves everyone as He loves us? That He longs for everyone to have faith in Him? If it does, then you are limiting your concept of God. He, and only He, because only He is God, has the love—the intensely personal love—to reach to you directly in your need, to reach to me in mine. To everyone in need everywhere. Of course, we can't conceive that. Why should we? We *give* love if we can forget ourselves long enough, but God *is* love.

23

Loving is not hard for Him. To love is His nature. The hard thing for God, I should think, is that we don't bother to *learn of Him*. We say prayers and perform kind acts and go to church and read our Bibles, but we concentrate on techniques and formulas and all sorts of doctrines—and then wonder why it is that we have so "little faith." We wonder why we have a kind of habit-faith with little or no life in it.

If you know you are asking from true need, with an open heart, do you need to beg and plead with the God who came in Person to show us that He means us all well? This is not to imply that it isn't all right to weep and plead with God if your heart is broken—but often our prayers have a kind of desperation that just does not indicate that confidence is there, too.

Knowing Him, as He is, will bring that confidence of itself. He is the "author and the finisher of our faith."

2

IS IT PRAYER?

I am fortunate enough I live in nearly ideal surroundings for writing. My house is not even on a public road. It
is im possible to "drive by." My land is edged by wide marsh
on three sides and woods on the other. Some years ago we
fought hard to protect the marshland and won, for the time
being anyway. Until the inevitable development moves a bit
nearer, the woods are still there.

And yet, when I truly need to rest, I leave home and go
to a motel where only my agent, my editor, and one friend
know the telephone number. I am not a recluse. I simply
work at home, and living as I do on St. Simons Island, Georgia, in a resort area, there are certain precautions I must
take. One of them, of course, is an unlisted telephone. But,
in case you've never had one, let me assure you that unlisted
telephones ring, too. My housemate and best friend, Joyce
Blackburn, and I have close friends and we love them. We

need to hear from our friends. We're as dependent as the rest of the human race on telephones. One of the most difficult adjustments I have to make when I'm writing historical novels is to remember that they did not have telephones in those days.

Lots of people have our unlisted number, by our choice. Of course, most don't. But when real rest is needed, in spite of the precautions, we pack up and leave the Island. Somehow I just don't rest unless I'm safely away even from the pleasant mail and the pleasant calls.

This is never true of God. He doesn't get tired, never needs rest, because He is God, the source of all energy. My love runs out when I'm overly tired. His can't. He is love.

Have you been struck, as I am this minute, that there is no one anywhere as available to everyone everywhere as is God?

And yet, just a few weeks ago someone said to me what I'd heard often in the past: "Oh, I can't just keep on bothering God with my dumb problems."

Now, that is really anthropomorphizing God. Bringing Him down to our size, our weakness, our inadequacy. Diminishing His love, His power, His energy, His minute-by-minute involvement with every person on earth. It sounds unselfish to hesitate to "bother God," perhaps, but it isn't. It's foolish even to think that God is ever too busy to attend to us. All that could be contained in a human being did come to earth in Jesus Christ, to live among us—to get into the chaos with us. Jesus did grow weary on earth because while He was God, He was also Man. While God's nature is completely knowable through Jesus, it was not limited even to that Life.

My beloved, late friend Dr. E. Stanley Jones used to say

that Jesus was "God's transformer." He bore in His person all that could be contained of the Almighty God (with never a contradiction in the quality of love), but in a form where the power could be grasped by a race of mere human beings. Raw electricity is not usable as it is. Before our houses can be lighted, that electricity must pass through a transformer. We could not survive direct exposure to it or use it otherwise.

God saw that people, His beloved creations, were not catching on to His true nature through all the years before Christ was born. Flashes of the truth penetrated certain earth minds, but far more clarification was needed. In His time God sent His Son, not only to redeem us from sin, but to show us once and for all His true nature. He came in a human body. He lived and worked and enjoyed His friends in a human body. He died in a human body. Then He rose again and even after death and resurrection. His disciples were still able to recognize Him.

We can grasp this kind of revelation of a Being other wise too vast, too powerful, too all-knowing. Revealing Him self in any other way had never been enough. Would never be enough. God knew human nature too well.

But Jesus, even in a man's body, did not minimize God, or limit Him as we do when we—in ignorance or false humility—declare Him to be too busy to hear us when we call. True, Jesus grew weary, drained at times, so that even He fled the crowds, got away from His own disciples, in order to renew Himself in the singular presence of His Father. But He always came back to *everyone*. Not once did He go into permanent hiding. They didn't find Him. *He came back to them.*

So far as we know, the only times Jesus went away by

Him self were the times when He needed to talk to His Father. To pray.

If conversation with the Father was necessary for the Son, isn't it an absolute necessity for us? And didn't Jesus reveal the Father to be totally available to everyone? When the dis ciples asked Him to teach them to pray. He went through no ritual, no formalities. He said simply and directly that they were to begin. To say directly, "Our Father . .

Over and over we are told that He said: "Ask and it shall be given you." He even urged us to use His name with the Father. ". . . whatsoever ye shall ask in my name, that will I do, that the Father may be glorified in the Son." And then He repeated it: "If ye shall ask anything in my name, I will do it."

Jesus has paved the way forever for us with the Father. He didn't merely indicate that He would allow us to ask in His name, He urged us to do it.

There is more in this urging, though, than the mere use of His name as a way to get the Father's attention. To pray in the name of Jesus is to pray *in His nature.*

For example, nothing in a single word He said would indi cate that we were to pray for someone else to get *his* or *her* "just punishment." In the midst of His own dark suffering on the cross Jesus prayed: "Father, forgive them, for they know not what they do." A nature such as that could never pray for revenge. Someone who loves me deeply, someone I love deeply—a longtime believer in Jesus Christ—said to me: "I can't help praying that the fellow who treated you so horribly will get his just due."

Thank heaven, God's "just due" is not like ours. If it were—if the justice of God were as faulty as ours—we'd all be in permanent trouble.

Jesus put this truth into unmistakable words: ". . . when ye stand praying, forgive, if ye have ought against any; that your Father also which is in heaven may forgive you your tres passes. But if ye do not forgive, neither will your Father which is in heaven forgive your trespasses." God simply *cannot* forgive an unforgiving heart.

Prayer, if it is true prayer, is not confined to particular words. Words may be read from a book and still be true prayer, but not necessarily. Prayer need be in no formed words at all. But prayer must be *in the nature* of the One who made it plain that the Father cannot forgive unless we also forgive those who have wronged us. It isn't that the Father is arbitrarily unwilling to grant the plea of an unforgiving heart. Doing so would harm us. He can't.

We are urged to pray in the name—the nature of Jesus Christ who lived out on the cross, His love—God's love—for enemies of all kinds. If we pray for revenge, if we have not ourselves forgiven, we simply cannot be praying in the nature of Christ.

"The prayer of a righteous man availeth much." What is a righteous man? To me a righteous man is no more than a redeemed man who is *not* self-righteous. One who gives no credit whatever to himself for his own goodness. Now, this isn't a matter of working at sounding humble when we pray. It is a matter of knowing the source of all true righteousness. To say, "If I'm righteous in any way, it is because God's right eousness has somehow worked its way through me," sounds like truth. It is truth. But only God knows if we really believe it. This is merely common sense. Because it seems to me that the righteousness of God is as different from mere human goodness as the justice of God is different from human justice.

We all know lots of "good" human beings. Good people who are not even believers in God. Some of the kindest, most charming people I've known are those who, when I mention that I'm a Christian, nod politely and with equal politeness attempt to change the subject. I have been treated with trickery and with enormous fairness by non-believing people and with trickery and enormous fairness by Christians. The point is not our nature, but His. Oh, part of the point is the sudden or gradual transforming of our natures, but we can get stuck on that, so that we lessen our need to discover God *as He really is.*

Prayer is both hard and easy. Jesus says all the gates are now open. We are free to say, "Our Father. . . Can the unrepentant man or woman say, "Our Father?" Yes. But he or she had better be prepared for an invasion of life- changing love if those words are spoken from the heart. The Father is alive and listening. . . and He is the same Father who revealed Himself in the Son who hung on a cross asking forgiveness for those who nailed Him there.

The same Father whose idea it was to send this Son in the first place, so that forever afterward no one, no one, could contend that God is remote, or too busy, or not interested out of all His mighty universe in the speck called Earth.

Christians are those who dare to believe that the God who began it all—the God who *is* the beginning—took the trouble to become one of us. Christians, if they have moved even a little beyond securing what they think of as their own eternal lives, are those who believe in a God who cares, with infinite love and compassion, for every human being who has or will live on the earth.

A God like this must, by His very nature, be approachable to anyone who needs Him. He is. He is the God who knew that unless He sent a part of Himself—a touchable, knowable, true part of Himself—to live among us, we would never really grasp His nature. It is not too hard to conceive of a powerful God. We love and at times, I think, nearly worship earthly power. We find it quite easy to aspire to it. Neither is it hard to conceive of an all-knowing God. It is possible for us to study, to cultivate our minds, until we possess awesome human knowledge. It is, unhappily, too easy for us—because of our faulty human natures—to conceive of a God of punish ment, a God of vengeance. The Father saw all this in us. Of course, He sees it now. But in His time, a time that we count as nearly two thousand years ago, He *did something about* our distorted concept of His own heart. His own intentions to ward us. He came Himself in the person of Jesus of Nazareth, who embodied the forgiving, loving, eternally caring Heart of the Father—before us, with us, so that we can pray; "Our Father . . ."

What the theologians call sinful men can, in a way, cope with a God of punishment—they can fight back. Government leaders burden the poor in order to stock military arsenals with still more weapons of overkill. Human nature loves a good fight. Man can cope with the concept of a vengeful God.

It's far easier for us to laugh at the hard luck of someone we dislike than it is to weep over the pain the misfortune is caus ing that person. Christians who proudly carry their Bibles almost everywhere they go are shocked at sin every day. Some of them condemn and shun the sinner. I will never forget an incident that happened many years ago, shortly after my own conversion to Jesus Christ, when a drunk young man was briskly ushered out of a church where I was to speak. I wanted to run after the drunk young man, to find out why he was there. I also wanted to run *from* those deacons who hurried him out. "We can't have people like that in God's house," they explained.

God would have welcomed the boy.

Strictly by God's grace and prodding that night, I eventually managed to show love to the men who had booted the young man out. What they did was not for me to judge. And I was just as unrealistic to be shocked by what the y did as they were to be shocked that the young man had dared to come to church while he was drinking. What they did gave me no license whatsoever to turn away from God. I admit to thinking that I couldn't follow their idea of God, but non believers who contend that they are "as good as the praying church people" have no solid ground on which to stand, ei ther. Jesus did not invite us to *be like* anyone else at all. He invited us to Himself. And when He said that we are all free to say, "Our Father." He meant it. But I couldn't pray that night until I had forgiven those well-to-do church deacons for what seemed to me an unchristian act.

Jesus meant that our access is wide open and that makes prayer easy. He also meant that we are to forgive and to pray knowing that whatever "righteousness" we have is God's goodness in us. And that makes prayer *hard*. We do so enjoy feeling that we are "good," or "right."

Prayer is hard also because too often we "pray" so that we can begin the day or go to sleep feeling we have done our "duty" to the Heavenly Father. And nine times out of ten we fall into that habit simply because wave been too busy to *think*. Thinking is not easy. Words flung in God's direction without thought or concentration may, for all I know, be heard. His is a constantly listening ear. Still, in the Old Testa ment, even before Christ came, people had learned that "the Lord looketh on the heart."

It's never too difficult to concentrate when we pray for a so lution to one of our personal problems. We quickly take time for that. We may even hasten for what God might be telling us to do in the situation. Our own problems are front and center in our minds. We are worried. Anxious. Worry and anxiety are strong attention-getters. It isn't "too much trouble" to pray standing in a hospital corridor outside a loved one's room. There, praying is all we can do. "I wish I could think of something more to do for you," we say, "but at least I can pray." What is more important? Why is prayer thought of as a last resort? The least we can do?

I don't think we really believe that about prayer, do you? Certainly we don't if we stop to think through the wonder in volved in it, the sheer wonder that anyone can, at any time, make direct contact with the Creator of the Universe. Why is it so easy to forget, or to grow casual about conversation with the Lord God?

One of the worst fears in my life before I became a believer at age thirty-three was that I might run dry as a writer, might never be able to think up   another plot, another idea,   for a radio or TV program. The fear haunted me. Well, not every idea, every plot, every characterization, I have come up with since I've known God has been good. But my fear is gone, because now I know that I have free and instant access to the source of all creativity. All day long at this typewriter I can stop and ask: "Lord, does that ring true? Is this too sarcastic? Is that too glib?"

I can always trust His taste, His perception, His criticism. Trust.

Is the important thing *what* we say to Him? *How* we say it? The *extent* of what we call our faith—as we petition

Him? No. What is most important is the identity of the One to whom we direct our petitions. What is important is *our knowledge* of the One to whom we pray.

If we really do think that He is too busy to bother with our small needs, there can be little trust. Little faith. My shoul ders and back hurt often when I write. In fact, they hurt most of the time. Muscle stiffness is one of the occupa- tional haz ards of being a writer. It's not only because of my age: I've had muscle pain when I work since I was thirty! I get so in volved in the work, I tense up. I'd like to know of a writer who doesn't do that. Do I dare ask God to "untense" me? To ease my aching shoulders and back? I surely do. Many, many times a day. And does He always do it? Well, He made my muscles the way they are and He knows how I get when I write. His answer often comes with a reminder to get up from the desk and take a few exercises. Don't I have sense enough to do that on my own? I suppose so, but I forget. Prayer is for us, too, you know. In asking God for help, we are often reminded of how to help ourselves. Paul said we were to "pray without ceasing." He didn't mean, of course, that we were to stop doing everything else. But God created us with the capacity for forming habits. There are good as well as bad ones. Prayer is a creative habit. A way of being.

Does this mean that we don't need to have times of con- cen trated, focused prayer? Of course not. But there are as many kinds, as many levels, of prayer as there are kinds and levels of thought.

Prayer is the pure privilege of being consciously with God. Of talking anything and everything over with Him. I, at least, have never thought of it as a duty. My *duty* is to pay my bills, meet manuscript deadlines, and dispatch my responsibilities.

My *privilege* is to talk to God. Not in order to please Him, but in order to be His friend. In another chapter we will speak more about being God's friend, but consider how long a human relationship would last if there was no communication between the two friends. How deep would a friendship send its roots if one person did all the talking and never listened to the others response?

On television the other day I saw a mind-shattering series of actual pictures of what we now call the Great Depression. When the program ended, I thought: "Lord, how could I dare claim that You have just answered that certain financial need I had when—even if You hadn't answered it—I still have had so much more than those people did? Am I off balance, Lord?

Am I so self-concerned? Am I cooking up an answered prayer so that I'll feel special to You? I know I'm no more special than those emaciated, hungry folk back in the nineteen thirties. I know that. Did You really answer my financial need recently? Or was it just luck? If You did—and

I think You did—why me? Why are there right now so many starving people whom You love as much as You love me?"

I waited. What came to me was this: "I can trust you, in part at least, to share what I just gave you. You don't share it as I wish you did, but you do share."

And instead of feeling generous and big-hearted, I vowed that I'd give away more—much more. Was I really in conver sation with God? I believe that I was. He knows for sure and I can leave that to Him.

I see nothing for any of us to do but leave a lot more to Him than we do now. The Christian life is a mystery. God

Himself, except as He has revealed His heart to us in Christ, is a mystery. Eternal life is a mystery. Eternal life after death and eternal life now. Even His revealed heart is a mystery in the sense that we can't conceive of His kind of love. We can only receive it and be changed by it and try, however feebly and ineptly, to pass it along.

Prayer is certainly a mystery. But it is, along with faith, one of God's dear gifts to us. Dear in the sense of being a treasure and dear in the sense of what our freedom to pray cost Him. Jesus Christ opened the Holy of Holies once and for all to anyone who chooses to enter.

3

IS IT GROWTH?

Matthew recorded the words of Jesus this way; "Consider the lilies of the field, how they grow; they toil not, neither do they spin: And yet I say unto you, That even Solomon in all his glory was not arrayed like one of these."

Luke recorded it this way: "Consider the lilies how they grow: they toil not, they spin not; and yet I say unto you, that Solomon in all his glory was not arrayed like one of these."

I happen to like the music in the Matthew version: ...they toil not, neither do they spin..." has a nice ring to it. But both say the same thing. The Lilies of the field grow, because they simply stand there meeting the conditions of growth. They depend solely upon God for their actual growing.

Does this mean that we have nothing to do in the process? Of course not. The lilies *do* meet the conditions of growth. They put their roots down into the earth for nourishment and they hold their leaves and flowers to the sun and rain. But they do not agitate. They do not struggle. They do not uproot themselves and race about the country hunting what might make them *feel* as though they're experiencing more growth.

A young man in his thirties wrote (and he is only one of many who write published authors such plaints) that he was absolutely sure that he would grow more quickly in his Christian life if only he could find a publisher for a book he had written. Others write that they are equally certain they will take gigantic leaps forward in their spiritual growth if only doors would open for them to enter what they call "full-time service."

I don't know a single Christian anywhere who is not supposed to be in full-time service to the God of love and redemption. In another chapter on service we will go more deeply into what it really means, but it means a lot more than preaching sermons or writing inspirational books or singing before an appreciative audience. All of these things can be a part of serving God, but they are not central. I am quick to admit that in retrospect, I see how smart God was to have me travel the country during the first decade of my Christian life. When I accepted a speaking date, I had to make some sort of attempt to communicate Him. This undoubtedly held me steady during those first unfamiliar years. But now, after thirty-three years as a follower of Christ, I do not consider those coast-to-coast tours or all the books I've written to have been more than a small part of my having met the conditions of growth.

They were met in the silence with God, when no one but God knew I was praying or reading my Bible or obeying. They were met in the daring moments when I chose to believe that the loved one just lost was not lost to me forever. They were met at the moments when, without fanfare, I chose God's way instead of my own.

What I once had to say from platforms was a *result* of growth in the hard places when I dared just to be still and meet some of God's conditions for my growth. When I dared to be a lily in the field. If the field is crowded with admiring people who exclaim: "Look at her—look at him—thats growth!"–no one can take credit. That's merely popular ap peal. I fully understand, but I also have to smile a little at the TV preachers–any preacher, any of God's people–who shout "humbly" about how many "decisions for Christ" they have persuaded others to make. I experience the same reac tion when they "give God all the glory" for the millions of dollars sent in by the saints as a result of *their* flourishing ministry. This is all bad? No. Not at all. It is simply not an authentic measure of spiritual growth. The fact is, all sorts of secular TV telethons bring in millions of dollars. People open their purses and give when their emotions are stirred.

The kind of growth we speak of here has nothing whatever to do with numbers or dollars. This kind of growth has solely to do with whether or not we are becoming more at home in the Presence of God Himself. Of God the Father, as anyone can know Him in Jesus Christ.

As *He is*.

Jesus said it as simply and as profoundly as it can be said: "I and the Father are one. If ye have seen me, ye have seen the Father." He also said that we are to forgive endlessly–again and again and again.

To me that means that no matter how hard we pray or serve or witness or praise, no matter how we struggle to grow, we wall not grow, we cannot, until we have forgiven *every one* for *everything*. There is no way to do that, humanly speaking, especially if we have been wronged. If it is true that we can never, never find a contradiction between Jesus Christ and the Father, we cannot expect to meet the conditions for growth with unforgiveness in our hearts, because Jesus made the need for forgiveness absolutely clear. A heart heavy with grudges and resentments and revenge will forever remain a stunted heart.

An eighty-six-year-old lady said to me yesterday; "Isn't it wonderful that we can grow a little every day?"

It is. But the mystery of growth is God's secret. We can set a plant in the sun and water it, but we cannot make it grow. The plant, with our help, simply meets the conditions of growth.

"Consider the lilies of the field, how they grow. . ."

Lilies stand there in the sun and the rain, their roots in the earth, and wait. Growth comes in God's time. Their part is to be there, meeting conditions.

Periods of spiritual growth are not always exhilarating, joy ous experiences. Actually, when real growth takes place, nine times out of ten we are not even aware that it is happening.

I am just emerging from such a period and only now do I realize that I have grown from it. It has been a genuine grow ing time, the nature of which I would never have chosen for myself. I got no glory from it, no praise, no credit. The growth, as it usually does, took place out of everyone's sight but God's. As it happened, few people gave me much thought at all during the entire ordeal. I sensed early that this was going to be true and so I stuck my roots as firmly as I knew how into the ground of my friendship with Christ and did my best to meet the conditions.

Some two months ago, as I write this, my only brother, Joe, died of cancer. As always, it seems, when a crisis strikes, I am either in the chaotic midst of a big manuscript, or almost at the always scary end of one. During the last pain-wracked week of my brother's life, I wrote page after page between long-distance calls from Mother, Joe's wife, Millie, and his daughter, Cindy. Most of what I wrote I had to toss in the wastebasket, but since I belong to a Redeemer God, I decided to redeem the time and try to work. Nothing was wasted. After taking four or five false directions in the manuscript, I began to know my main character as I probably wouldn't have known him otherwise.

When Joe was finally released from his suffering, I drove north over the mountains to be with Mother for the services. I adored my brother. An hour after I knew he was gone, I began to realize how much I'd unconsciously depended upon always having him. The enormous weight of my mother's grief rolled onto mine and soon outweighed it. In the silence with God, as my friend Joyce drove me to Mother's house, I listened when He reminded me that I couldn't carry my own grief alone and certainly not Mother's. The first morning on the road I was swamped when I awoke with Millie's grief. What a difficult man to lose! Joe's humor, his smile, his singular lilt, could never, never be replaced—not for any of us. But Millie would miss him more than anyone. For all the years of their marriage her life had revolved around his. In the car, still heading north that second day, without realizing it, I managed to meet another condition of growth. I agreed wholly with the Lord that I couldn't carry Millie's grief, either. Now, the word growth—or the phrase "meeting the conditions of

41

growth"—did not come to mind. I wasn't hunting for a way to grow spiritually. We seldom grow when we try. I was just hunting for a way to cope.

After three weeks away from writing my novel, I came back to my desk and met another condition unconsciously. I was only aware of having made the decision once and for all that I couldn't carry my grief or anyone else's and still finish that book. With all my heart I longed to call Joyce into my office, to call my editor, to call Mother—to say that I couldn't write, that I simply had to have a rest. That the grief on top of all those endless months of work on the long, long novel was too much. Had I said that, everyone would have encouraged me to stop work, to get away. No one did because I didn't stop. I had God's word for it that I wasn't going to have to carry more than my work. The "yoke became easy." *He was in it with me.* He knew better than I how important it was for me to finish that rough draft on time. He knew—I certainly don't—what other crisis may lie ahead. "Be good to yourself," a friend said. "Get away and do nothing for a month."

By the time she said that, I had no need to do anything but write. It was then that I realized—and quite suddenly—that I 'd grown a bit from the heartbreak. I had done nothing con sciously to grow. I hadn't thought of the word *growth.* One just doesn't at a time like that. But evidently I had met the only condition necessary—I took God at His word.

He said that He would be with me always. Always includes during my grief, my panic over the unfinished manuscript, the months ahead when I knew I'd be trying to comfort Mother and Millie and Cindy. I was about one month of hard work away from the end of the book.

My realization at the end of that month that I had not only finished the manuscript, but had grown in the process, has been proven right. During the next week I answered or no tated more than fifty letters, and then began the writing of this book. I had at least grown a bit stronger.

Some grief is so sharp it prevents us from working. But when we can bring ourselves to meet the one condition of growth–to stand, like the lilies, in the strength of God's love when the storms beat down—*we will grow.*

Let me repeat: We don't grow much when we're trying too hard. When we really take a firmer root, we don't dwell on it. The bud doesn't struggle against its brown casing in spring. It stays in position and grows and after a time the brown casing drops away.

Growth is God's department. This is true for leaves in the spring, for crocuses in the snow, and for people.

One sure sign of spiritual growth, as I see it, is the ability to resort to humor when what we really want to do is hit someone. I hold strong political views. God goes on protect ing me from being an out-and-out extremist, but I have come by my views on my own, from listening, from reading, from keeping up on current events, from watching governments come and go, from not rationalizing away the suffering world.

At the moment my political beliefs are definitely not being implemented. Well, that's all right. If any country went from election to election always with the same party winning, we'd grow lopsided. As much as I disagree with things now— all the way from the loss of environmental protection to the theory that we will regain our economic health by stepping on the necks of the poor, to the seeking of "peace" through still more nuclear weapons—perhaps this present trend, when it ends, and trends always do end, will create a better balance.

Not long ago I was introduced to one of the most delightful women I've met in many years. I meet so many people that I don't always let my feelings be known, for fear I can't keep up with another correspondence or another relationship. This time I relaxed and enjoyed! And then, during our second or third meeting, I discovered that she was as far on the opposite side from me politically as anyone could be. Did it ruin everything for me? No. Would it have ruined everything for me a short time ago? Yes. And that would have been true because of what I'm like when I look away from God even briefly. When our political disagreement surfaced and I found myself laughing at *me*, I got another inkling of my growth. I wasn't struggling to learn how to disagree politely. By nature I enjoy a political argument too much. But the God I follow loves Republicans as much as He loves me and I simply faced it. Humor surfaced and the friendship holds.

If we nurture a prejudice of any kind, we stunt our growth in God. Prejudice is prejudging before we find out what it is really like to be the other person. We're all guilty of it. Any church member who fails to tolerate someone with whom he or she disagrees stunts growth. There isn't any need to compromise what we believe in order to be kind to another person who happens not to see things exactly as we see them. I could no more pull a trigger on a gun and send a hot bullet into the graceful, wild, free body of a deer than I could fly off my upstairs balcony. It took a while, but I came to accept the (for me difficult) fact that my brother and father reveled in hunting deer. As I matured, I accepted them as they were— both preferring guns to books.

And that is the key: As we mature. *As we grow.*

My beloved friend Anna B. Mow taught me many years ago that maturity is learning to make choices. It is up to us. We choose whether to come down on the side of our preju dices and preferences or to make our choices in the growth-inducing ground of God.

Every bad habit of thought or mind or body to which I still cling is immaturity on my part. I cannot make myself grow, but only I can meet the conditions of growth. And we choose. We decide.

I know hundreds of people who run from retreat to retreat, from conference to conference, trying desperately to grow in God. This does happen. I have seen enormous growth take place in one week's time when open-minded and open-hearted men and women meet together in God's Presence—if they honestly want to grow. But I still say that most real growth, the kind that stands us in good stead when the crises strike, is far more likely to come about when we aren't even thinking of growing. Have you never felt impelled to write a certain letter or make a certain tele-phone call, but decided to wait until morning before doing it? Have you never held a letter overnight and torn it to bits in the morning light? What made you do that? You slept. Whether you knew it or not, you made a God-like choice of sleeping on it first—you went to sleep leaving it up to God to guide you. As you slept, perhaps you grew. In the morn-ing you saw a saner way out.

Every transaction, however seemingly inconsequential, made consciously in the Presence of the Lord God adds something of value to the core of our beings. No one else needs to know a thing about it. Most of the time it's better if no one but God does know. But every small victory, every choice in His direction, brings growth.

"I am the vine, ye are the branches," Jesus said.

I once asked myself: "Did you ever hear a branch plead with the vine to send more sap? No, the branch just stays in position and—grows. Growth is the vine's responsibility." Our part is to stay in position.

Does growth really matter? It matters endlessly. I fully ex pect us to keep on growing throughout Eternity because we will be in the Presence then of Life Himself. For now, we are to "consider the lilies of the field, how they grow." And we are to remember that even Solomon's beautiful garments can not hold a candle to them.

4

IS IT PRAISE?

The psalmist wrote: "Let everything that hath breath praise the Lord."

Does praise really matter? Oh, yes, but exactly what is it?

Is it that occasional exalted feeling of a Sunday morning when, with the practiced help of a choir of voices, we lift our own? Is it merely remembering to devote a portion of our prayer time to what we think of as praise? Is it the surge of emotion, spirit, joy, during the final elevating strains of a Vivaldi concerto? Is it remembering, or going back to re-read, Edna St. Vincent Millay's magical line about God's having "made the world too beautiful this year"? Is praise the recognition of beauty?

As I write, I can see the coastal morning sun picking out a wild flight of yellow grapevines across trees and forest bushes, literally stringing light through the gloom of the dense woods at the foot of my lawn. I can see my eccentric mockingbird flash by and land possessively on a branch laden with bright red holly berries. I can see the shapes of one long-leafed pine and one live oak black-shadowed across the fading fall grass in the yard. Strands of clean, airy gray Spanish moss wave under the sun and a small breeze. I can walk down the hall and into my friend Joyce Blackburn's rooms at the other end of our house and see there, dazzling my eyes, the Frederica River twisting its serpentine way through the wide marsh, and the same golden autumn light *shouts—beauty*. "Oh, Lord, I do fear thou hast made the world too beautiful this year!"

My heart swells, my spirit lifts, my wonder grows.

If I stop work long enough really to look, to let the sights penetrate my emotions, reach all the way to my intellect, I think: The God I follow thought up all this beauty! How I wish I knew *how* to let Him know what the sight of it does for me.

Last night we spent a long, important evening listening, almost wordlessly, to music. To our favorite Vivaldi concerti, to a magnificent album of Bach, to the late Kathleen Ferrier singing Brahms's "Contralto Rhapsody." We don't talk often when we listen to music that matters. Actually, we are both annoyed by mere sound in the background, much preferring silence unless there is music that matters. Background tunes in supermarkets and doctors' offices may soothe some. They bother me. But last evening, when a passage stirred one of us in particular, we would say: "That just *has* to be the music of heaven! Thank You, Lord, for thinking up music."

Was that praise?

Is it a desire to praise that causes me to long for more skill with words when I try to communicate to you what

I sense as I look at one bright slash of crimson where my single tupelo tree stands turning as red as blood in the otherwise dark woods?

Is it praise when what might have been a bad situation turns out well and we murmur: "Thank You"?

Is it true praise when exchanged looks cause understanding to become tangible? Is the resultant quick quiet in the heart true praise for that understanding?

Or do we tend to confuse praise with gratitude? Are they not the same? The longer I think about that question, the more convinced I am that the only logical answer is yes and no.

When my mother looked out the window beside the chair where she sat for the last years of her life, she saw no sunlight in the woods, no expanse of October blue sky, no fringed shadows on the grass. She lived in a city where physical sight is hemmed in by neighbors' houses, a high-rise apartment, the garage next door. Oh, she saw beauty— her neighbor, Mary Jane Goshom, kept blooming plants in her windows for Mother to see. Mary Jane's small city garden did its very best. Mother, in turn, kept blooming geraniums on the side stoop so that Mary Jane would have beauty, too. But they were city-bound, and now and then, I could almost not bear the beauty I see from every window in my house because they couldn't see it. Should city dwellers, then, not bother with praise? Am I really praising God when my heart lifts at the sight of sun and shadow and green woods and blue sky or am I simply enjoying, as anyone with sight would naturally enjoy, the views from my house in the woods?

Does any of this really matter?

Do you ever think that a singing bird might be praising

God? Ornithologists insist that birds sing only for mating purposes— to scare off other birds in the territory or to attract each other. Maybe so, but I *like* to think my cardinals and towhees and painted buntings and mockingbirds are praising Life itself, and that's all right, too. "Let *everything* that hath breath praise the Lord."

God is never as rigid as are some of his more intense followers. He created every living thing, especially us, to enjoy–up to capacity. More and more I believe that we are ungrateful when we don't do all in our power and His to increase our capacities to enjoy.

But is praise gratitude? Is gratitude praise?

On the yes side, in the purest sense, praise and gratitude are one, if we know God. Now, that is not to be mistaken for a rigid statement of religious doctrine. Anyone can experience true gratitude no matter what he or she believes. Even the troubled person pronounced a criminal by his society can be thankful for a shorter prison term or for a life sentence in-stead of death at the hands of fellow human beings who have decided that he or she no longer has the right to live. I knew gratitude for many things in my own life before I knew Christ. And although I directed my gratitude toward luck, or my own talent, I often felt what I recognized as gratitude. I was grateful to my parents who went on believing in me and supporting me with money and faith until I succeeded in a measure as a writer. I was grateful then and I go on being grateful every day that I can earn my living doing the only thing I could or would want to do.

Gratitude matters, whether or not we walk in relationship with God, because it is an exercise good for the soul. But is it only the beginning of praise? Can gratitude *become* praise when it is focused on the Person of the living God?

To me this *focus* is integral to praise.

The kind of praise to which the Bible urges us is always—not sometimes, but always—directed away from ourselves toward God. We are to "praise the Lord" for being Himself. Do we sometimes fall into an unwitting trap here? Do we use the phrase "Praise the Lord" sometimes from mere habit? When we feel we ought to say it? When, perhaps unconsciously, we are using it to camouflage some indirect boasting about ourselves? Do we now and then say, "Praise the Lord," when what we really mean is "Praise me"? I watch this tendency in myself the way a kingfisher watches for his breakfast on the banks of a river or a lake.

For example: I want someone to know how hard I've worked, how many long hours I've spent at this typewriter on a certain manuscript. I want to vent my pride of accomplishment and so I say: "The Lord was so good. I finished the big rough draft of my current novel on time—even after the weeks away from my desk when my brother and then my mother died."

What's wrong with that? Nothing, really. Wasn't the Lord good to have helped me concentrate, to have convinced me that my separation from my brother is only temporary? Yes. Shouldn't I have praised Him? Yes. But only that same Lord knows whether my words carried pride in myself along with praise.

All right, you say, but shouldn't you have given God some credit for all that concentration? Didn't your own health remain good until you finished? Didn't He create the mind you used to assemble and integrate all those historical facts into your plot? Yes. And surely, there is nothing wrong with recognizing and admitting one's own fulfillment in a job completed—to be thankful to God. So what's the problem? Isn't self-deprecation spiritually pompous? If there's anything that strikes me as spiritual pomposity, it is for someone to deprecate himself or herself after a job well done, hoping to sound spiritual or humble. The Lord is not fooled either way. He knows when we're boasting under the guise of praise to Him and He also knows when we've done our part in that piece of work. Self-deprecation and boasting are both forms of unhealthy ego. To tell someone of our gratitude to God for health and the energy to work is right on center, but to me at least, it is not pure praise. Praise is gratitude moving beyond itself to God *as He is*.

Does real praise, then, always involve gratitude? I believe it does. Gratitude does not necessarily involve praise, but praise—true praise—springs naturally from gratitude. Praise goes deeper. When we praise, we have moved beyond gratitude for divine favor or protection. Praise moves outward. We pour out om' adoration when we praise. Praise is directed away from us toward God himself. When we truly praise, we become absorbed in the object of our praise.

Deeply felt gratitude for one particular gift moves from the gift and our joy in it to the Giver. That seems to me to be real praise. When our praise moves away from the gift to the Giver, we give God joy. Is this true? Gan we really give God joy? The Bible says: "He will rejoice over thee with singing." God singing over me? Over you? Yes. If we feel too lowly, too much a worm for God to sing over, then were insulting the Creator. He thought us up in the first place, exactly as we are. He may be the only one who can rejoice over us, sing over us, but He can. He sees our potential in Him. His capacity for joy is beyond anything we can begin to comprehend. Just as His capacity for suffering is beyond anything we could endure.

Words often block real praise. If that surprises you, how many people do you know who will say, "Praise the Lord," at the drop of a hat and without thinking? Just as we can repeat the Lord's Prayer without thinking about one single word, so can we fall into the dulling habit of repeating, "Praise the Lord." I say it, but I've never allowed it to become a careless habit because I don't believe anyone is that constant in praise. Of all phrases, "Praise the Lord" should not become a cliche. Think for a minute of your own reaction after all this time to "Have a nice day."

Praise, if it is real, must be honest. Noise, whether it is repetition of "Praise the Lord" or clanging cymbals, is not necessarily praise. It can be. Loud singing can be praise, but it isn't praise because it's loud. I don't know about you, but I've experienced deep moments of what I am able to recognize more readily as real praise, alone and in the silence, without words. Now, words are fine when we praise. We need them usually. Music, poems, Scripture, verbal prayers, all are useful. They are not needed, not essential, but they do help us concentrate.

One of my most meaningful experiences in praise came a year or so ago, as I write this, when my friend and housemate, Joyce Blackburn, was writing and collecting her small, potent *Book of Praises*. I happened to be writing a novel at the time, but the months during which she read and made se lections and wrote her own glowing poems of praise were il luminated for me as I worked. I would be beating away at this typewriter, oblivious of the entire twentieth century, when gradually I'd sense someone in the room. After a week or so I began to know what to expect. Joyce and I are such compatible friends that she can interrupt me with anything, for any reason, and I don't feel interrupted. Our life is all of a piece. I also know that she came and stood in my doorway, waiting for me to look up, only when she'd found something she just couldn't keep to herself. I looked forward to her every appearance, because I knew she'd discovered something which would undoubtedly turn on my own praise tap. And I need to praise when I'm trying to untangle dates and events in a novel set in an earlier time in history.

"Listen to this," she'd say, and then read what she'd found:

> In one salutation to thee, my God, let all my senses spread out and touch this world at thy feet. Like a raincloud of July hung low with its burden of unshed showers, let all my mind bend down at thy door in one salutation to thee.
> Let all my songs gather together their diverse strains into a single current and flow toa sea of silence in one salutation to thee. Like a flock of homesick cranes flying night and day back to their mountain nests, let all my life take its voyage to its eternal home in one salutation to thee.
>
> RABINDRANATH TAGORE

Another time, she read from the great American scientist George Washington Carver:

> When I touch that flower,
> I am touching infinity.
> *I learn what I know*
> By watching and loving
> Everything.

There was more, and each passage moved me, in the

midst of work, to silent praise. Of course, I was inevitably refreshed. Often, after Joyce had gone back to her own desk, I'd sit here and look out at the edge of the woods—learning what I know, "by watching and loving." Praise came naturally, with no effort and almost always no words on my part.

Praise, to me, is the simple, pure essence of just being-with Him.

What does the "sacrifice of praise" mean?

The Old Testament reference to "the sacrifice of praise" was, as I understand it, a particular ritual of praise. A literal offering that Jehovah understood. Since Christ has come, a true "sacrifice of praise" may be anything from the gift of our wills when everything in us cries *no!*, to the acceptance of the death of a loved one.

I have seen many people offer "the sacrifice of praise." Their offerings brought praise to my heart. At the funeral home my brother's wife, Millie, beside his casket, made a "sacrifice of praise" which I will never, never forget. Most im portant, Millie was not aware that she was doing anything that could remotely be called "a sacrifice of praise." She did, though, and if no one else benefited, I did. My memories of my brother will always be shot through with good times and laughter. He was a fun-man, with superb wit and humor. Like his sister, he had a few tics about things that made no sense whatever. For years we laughed together at certain idiosyncrasies of our grandmother, who lived with us during our childhood. We laughed at other things, too, which probably would have amused no one else. That day, beside his still body, Millie, whose humor matched his, laughed softly, and said, "I guess it's a good thing Joey's in heaven, because now he won't mind that baby's breath quite so much. I begged the florist not to put baby's breath in any of his flowers. Look at that I know he's laughing."

Every basket and spray of flowers was riddled with baby's breath. I dislike the stuff, too. A bunch of baby's breath alone might be light and airy, but when I want roses, I want only roses. So did my brother. Millie made her "sacrifice of praise" when she allowed God to give her a moment's release from grief. To give me a moment's release, too. We laughed. It was real laughter. Our laughter praised the living God in whose presence this beloved man now lives fully. When Millie reads this she will be surprised that what she said struck me as a "sacrifice of praise." It did. Real praise.

In Jeremiah 33 :10 ,11—where you can find the phrase "sacrifice of praise"—it is depicted as coming, along with the voice of joy, *out of desolation*. Perhaps there is a way for you, for me, to show God "a sacrifice of praise" out of happiness. I doubt it. Praising God when we're happy, when everything goes well, is easy. There's no sacrifice involved. We often forget to praise Him when life is good, but when we do remember, it certainly isn't hard. My sister-in-law made her "sacrifice of praise" that day *out of desolation*. But I, at least, heard the "voice of joy" in her sacrifice. Happiness fades at the graveside of a loved one. God's joy does not. It holds.

My friend Joyce read many praise-inducing passages to me during the months in which she worked on her *Book of Praises*. I can pick up the book now at any time, and do, especially when I don't feel like praising—and praise comes. My heart opens.

Gratitude and praise are the joint keys that unlock the bolted heart. Gratitude, and especially praise. If a heart is grateful and full of praise, it cannot be closed. Even Almighty

God cannot adjust or heal a closed heart. Jesus Christ does not, according to the way He carefully explained it, batter down doors: "Behold, I stand at the door and knock. If any man hear my voice and open the door, I will come in." He waits for an open heart, and I know of no better way to pry open even the tightest heart than with gratitude and praise.

Praise will follow gratitude, if one knows God personally, because of what He is really like. And gratitude and praise do matter. They are the keys to our hearts.

In her *Book of Praises* Joyce Blackburn wrote this poem. I read it almost every day.

> *Let everything that hath breath praise the Lord,*
> Because you are alive, you can respond!
> Praise is response,
> the voluntary response
> of our total selves
> or even a part of ourselves
> to the presence and doings of the Lord,
> Creator-Redeemer-God.
> Praise is the astonishment we express
> when touched by his Infinity,
> by his intimacy,
> by his attention concentrated on each one of us.
> Praise is the silence of awe we feel
> when we recognize a miracle,
> the wholeness we feel
> in the arms of Almighty Love,
> the freedom we know,
> once captured, changed, kindled.
> Let us respond
> to the One

in whom we live
and move
and have our being.
Let us praise the Lord.

5

IS IT SERVICE?

This is a chapter which needs to be written and read with care and concentration. The word *service* in what we think of as God's work has, for most, a hallowed ring. We revere those who, especially in the past, worked for little compensation beyond a job well done for Him. Evangelists, teachers, doctors and nurses, parish priests and pastors, worked often only for their food and a place to sleep, little more. As always, Jesus used a colorful metaphor for Christian service: "The fields are white to harvest, but the laborers are few."

Given the multiplying needs in our world, the laborers—those who work because they love—are still few. Those who serve God as their professional calling are now compensated more realistically, but still more is expected of them because of it. I have heard ministers say that they are required to do so much paperwork, to spend so much time fund-raising and heading up organizations, that being a shepherd, in the sense that Christ urged, is almost the last thing they manage to do. Some complain that most days they don't feel like ministers, because in truth they are administrators. Others confide in me in a puzzled way, wondering if somehow they are really serving God in the true sense. The administrative aspect of a cleric's life is, of course, the reason why large churches hire a staff of ministers. I have no valid comment about any of this. I have always been a writer. I work for God in the sense that I try to live for Him, but I am free of such complex problems as those carried by ministers of organized churches. I once spent a lot of time in the air and on trains and behind the wheel of my car, moving from one speaking engagement to another. I no longer do that, because my writing schedule has become too confining. But even when I did travel much of the year, I did it on my own. I made my own schedule. Of course, when I had a cold or felt ill for any reason, I didn't have a substitute, but I can only commend the men and women who manage to serve God within the limitations and burdens of an organization.

"Finding time for my own personal devotional time is the most difficult of all," one priest told me. A Protestant minister wrote not long ago that he doesn't preach on prayer anymore from his pulpit on Sunday because he doesn't feel he takes the time to pray as he should. "I spiel off names to God on the run," he admitted.

Even in the simplicity and relative freedom of my own life as a writer, I understand feeling hurried and pushed. I am overly conscientious, some tell me, about answering my mail. Maybe I am, but no one ever explains how to handle my bad conscience over those unanswered letters. Often readers write to commend me for my "service to God."

Well, those letters invariably cause me to think. You see, I have never thought of myself as being in what is called "full-time Christian service." I still don't. I simply earn my living by writing books. Yet, if I wrote even a novel without God in it, I'd be so bored I'd never finish the manuscript. The nonfiction books I write, with the exception of a few autobiographical pieces, are plainly about living the Christian life. Back in 1949 I became a follower of Jesus Christ, so how could I write about living without mentioning Him?

But my one goal—almost from the beginning—has been to be a friend to Christ, not to serve Him. Not long ago a sportswriter from a big-city paper did an article on my love of baseball. The headline above a photograph of me tossing a baseball to my favorite Atlanta Braves player read: "God's Friend Burns One Over!"

The headline made me feel silly. The pleasant young man who interviewed me had asked an outsized number of ques tions about my relationship with God considering that he was writing a sports story about a past-middle-aged woman who loves baseball enough to spend her annual vacation in the same place the Atlanta Braves take spring training. I liked him and so I spoke freely of my walk with Christ. Not speak ing freely of it, if asked, seems false to me. At one point he asked me if I thought of myself as being in "full-time Chris tian service." I calmly answered, "No. I just try to be God's friend." I didn't consider that headline material.

And that brings me to what I want carefully to say here. It is a marvelous thing to be in His service and it is an equally marvelous thing to try to be His friend. To those of us who were not formally trained in theology, especially to those of us who have not attended schools where Christian service is stressed, it may simply be easier to understand an attempt to be God's friend. One thing is certain: if I am His friend to any degree, if I am peaceful in His Presence, if I stay in con scious contact with Him, I am *not* damaging His work or His reputation.

One night, many years ago, I spoke in a church some- where on the West Coast, and the minister asked me to do some- thing I really didn't know how to do. I hadn't been a Chris- tian very long and hadn't, at that time, been in a church where a specific invitation to accept Christ was giv- en. But be- fore I spoke that night, this nice gentleman asked me if I'd give an invitation when I finished. In my way I did. And then I sat down while the choir sang. As I remember, some young people responded. But what I recall so clearly is that the friend who was traveling with me, who *had* been trained in an evangelical school, said with amazement: "You just said what you had to say and sat down. You didn't even look worried that maybe no one would respond!"

I didn't look worried because I wasn't. I am one hundred percent in favor of everyone knowing Christ. More truth- fully, I am in favor of everyone waking up to the fact that whether we know Him or not. He has always known us. The so-called "search for Christ" is an interesting contradiction. If God knows everything, and if He really came to earth saying "Fol low me," would He then turn around and hide from anyone under any circumstance?

I am still excited when I receive a letter or hear that some one has turned to Christ after reading one of my books; but before God, it has nothing to do with me—and that is not "humble talk." I write what I truly believe, what I have expe- rienced, and the rest is up to Him. In the tight places in my life I try to be His friend. It is now habit for me to remem- ber that since so many millions of people know that I call myself a Christian, I have the reputation of Jesus Christ in my hands at all times. That sentence appears in much of my other writing. There is no way it wouldn't, because I believe it so utterly. If a long-distance operator is in a bad mood, and I long to ask why he or she doesn't try Tums, I remember His reputation instead. I'm not trained to serve God in specialized ways, but I or anyone else can make an effort to *be His friend.*

Clerics and missionaries and evangelists are not all saints. Becoming a professional "worker for Christ," no matter how many degrees may be tacked on after one's name, does not make anyone God's friend, on whom He can count. Actually, I've met only a few persons in my long life on whom I thought God could truly depend under any circumstance. The two who come to mind were in "full-time Christian service," but neither made much of it. One was the late world-famous Methodist evangelist and statesman Dr. E. Stanley Jones. The other is my dear, dear friend, author-missionary Dr. Anna B. Mow. Both were formally trained to do God's work, but nei ther was a professional religioso!

I hope you'll think that through. Stanley Jones was, and Anna Mow is, first of all, God's friend. I could tell Stanley Jones anything and count on his continuing love and under standing for me. He, like Anna, was absolutely *not shockable.* I could pick up my telephone right now, call Anna, and tell her things I otherwise might only tell God. This is rare with any human being. It is not at all unusual where God is con cerned. If He could be shocked, He wouldn't be God. Anna Mow and I do not agree on every small thing, but she loves me with all the human love God can supply and she encour ages me to *think for myself.* As does God. Every telephone conversation with her is more like watching a child open pres ents on Christmas morning than a talk with an eighty-nine-year-old "retired" missionary. Perhaps I should have said "the usual concept of an eighty-nine-year-old re-tired missionary." She is still ranging the world—not just America—the world, speaking and writing about the God who keeps her in perpet ual wonder that she has the privilege of being *His friend*. I have never once heard her mention numbers or crowd sizes or any other "fruit of her labors." The only thing she wants to talk about, even when she's exhausted from jet lag, is what wonders God is doing. Anna is caught up in her friendship with Christ, and when she literally enters His Presence one of these days, she will be able to dry my tears in a hurry be cause I already know a little of what the extent of her joy will be.

Is Anna a servant of God? Of course she is. Was Stanley Jones God's servant? Yes. But first of all there was the divine friendship. Neither person, to my knowledge, ever *tried* to be like God. They had it too straight for that. Their friendship with Him was healthy throughout. He was the Almighty Other to them both. They wasted no effort trying to imitate Him. Anna gives little if any thought to serving Him. Love for Him long ago overcame her desire to be even a good servant.

Anna has her own human frailties straight, too. She isn't perfect. Stanley Jones would laugh at the thought. Anna does laugh at it. She knows for certain that she is—along with the rest of us—still on her way. But the way is Jesus Himself.

Joyce Blackburn's mother and father were the minister and minister's wife of modest Baptist churches for more than half a century. Audry, the minister's wife, will tell you that it took her a while, but she finally agreed with her husband, Leroy, that their lives belonged to the people they were sent to serve. This included getting up in the middle of the night if a drunk man or woman rang their telephone. It included going to that person—even mopping up if need be—and telling no one. Joyce remembers that on Sunday morning after Sunday morning when she was a child her father bathed, dressed in his pulpit clothes, and preached on less than two hours sleep because he had been sitting with someone until time to die, or sitting with someone too drunk to remember that the minister was there. The Blackburns were *God's friends*.

Through correspondence I have come to know a young lady in Maine who has spent the past ten or fifteen years of her life caring for severely retarded, deformed children in her own home. When Kathy first began to write to me, she was in a tangle of self-pity about everything life had to offer. For some reason I kept in touch. Then, after a few years, without any big declaration of newfound faith or transformation, she was writing about the retarded children she and her mother had taken in. I believe Kathy Woodbury now has seven of these children. She sends pictures of them— she loves them with her whole being—and some of the little faces are too ter rible to dwell on. It has been so long since I've heard Kathy complain about her own lot in life, I had almost forgotten that self-pity prompted her very first letter all those years ago. She and her wonderful mother and husband are too busy being God's friends. If you asked if they were in Christian service, they would give you a quizzical look. Kathy is mar ried now to a beautiful young man who shares her love of these children. Now, in Bangor, Maine, God has at least three friends, each very busy at His singular profession of loving.

God has friends, real friends, both in and out of profes sional Christian service, whose life focus is to return His love. This is an impossible goal unless one has experienced at least one blinding moment of realization of the quality of His love for all of us. An unadorned realization of His love is a blind ing experience. Everything false and acquired and comfort able is stripped away: The dark side of all human nature confronts us and it is our own. But thank God—and only God could manage this—we are shown at the *same instant* the na ture of that Love flowing from the Cross where Goodness Himself died for our sake. If any human being were forced to look at the darkness in himself or herself without seeing that Love at the same moment, only horror would result.

Serving God because you are God's friend puts a perma nent end to duty. A lady told me at the store the other day that she wouldn't miss church on Sunday for anything. "I feel so much better when I go. I can begin the week then knowing I've done my duty by God."

That wouldn't get me within a mile of a church!

Life is riddled with enough duties, things we have to do or else. I confess I admire anyone who can stick it out for duty's sake. I couldn't. I wouldn't. Books have been written about men and women who entered religious life as professionals and lived out their lives in duty to God. They are better peo ple than I. But let me glimpse the nature of His Love—let me think for even one minute that the young Man hung there on His Cross with His arms stretched wide for love's sake–and I'm His.

Does service matter? Yes. As with all chapters in this book, service matters. I serve my best friend, with whom I live. She serves me. If I didn't love her, though, if I weren't her friend, I'd find a way out of the serving in no time.

In case you think any part of this chapter is my own original thought, it isn't. I got it from the words of Jesus. And I'll never forget when I first caught His meaning—at least, some of it. I was exhausted from a travel and speaking schedule that was too heavy. The people who drove me to my train (this was long ago) knew they had piled on the engagements far beyond what they'd promised and the last thing the gentleman said was: "God will rest you. After all, you're His ser vant."

I must have been in Portland, Oregon, because I distinctly remember sitting in my seat by the window as the train moved past the dark, almost frightening beauty of the Cum berland River Gorge. My mood was as dark as the Gorge. On the train east I had to write five chapters of a book due at the publisher almost as soon as I got home. I had a small portable typewriter, but no energy for writing. As always, when I'm at the end of myself for any reason, I turned to the Gospel of John, this time to chapter 15, where I knew Jesus spoke of the comforting fact that He is the vine and we are the branches. Branches, as we've already said, only have to stay attached to the vine. The vine supplies the energy and nourishment. I read on to verse 13 and there it was:

> Greater love hath no man than this,
> that a man lay down his life for *his friends*.

I turned from the book and looked out the train window. Something had begun to stir in me. I read on:

Ye are my friends, if ye do whatsoever I command

you. Henceforth *I call you not servants*; for the servant knoweth not what his lord doeth: *but I have called you friends*; for all things that I have heard of my Father I have made known unto you.

Suddenly I was so excited, I could have climbed the steep Walls of the Cumberland River Gorge! The well-meaning gen tleman at the train station had said I was *serving* God. That implied that I hoped at all times to please the God I served and that when I felt inadequate, as I had that day when I had been too weary to speak well, I was a failure. I had failed the Divine One for whom I worked. So, maybe I didn't speak very well or very clearly. I was tired, but right there in black and white I had Jesus' own word for it that He no longer called me servant—He called me *friend*. Friends forgive friends when they fail, when they grow weary. I didn't need to feel a failure.

I fell soundly asleep sitting up in the train seat and slept five wonderful hours. Then I read the passage again and real ized that He not only released me from the "job" of trying to be a good servant, He explained why He'd done it. " . . . for the servant knoweth not what his lord doeth: but I have called you *friends*; for *all things* that I have heard of my Fa ther I have made known unto you." The italics are mine, but they matter. When I 'm confused by events or doctrinal inter pretation or any perplexing dogma, I need only to check it against what Jesus said and I'll know. If He didn't mention it, I don't need to worry.

Scholarly theologians have called me Christo-centric for years, but that's all right. I 'm responsible for my life and they for theirs. If I can only understand God's intentions through Jesus Christ, I'm still in pretty good company. Remember, the beloved disciple John said: "In the beginning was the Word, and the Word was with God, and the Word was God. . .

And the Word was made flesh, and dwelt among us No man hath seen God at any time; the only begotten Son, which is in the bosom of the Father, he hath declared him."

All the disciple John needed to know in order for his heart to rest when he wondered about the true nature of the Fa ther, he had found in Jesus.

And Jesus said that He no longer called us servants. *He calls us friends.* Are we good friends to Him? At times, but if He took responsibility for faulty human beings like those who followed Him about the dusty roads of His land, what earthly or heavenly reason do we have to believe that He will do less with us? He even takes the responsibility for the friendship.

Most of those called, or who call themselves God's servants, are—whether they've thought about it or not—*His friends.*

Serving Him certainly does matter. Being His friend, to me, matters even more.

6

IS IT GIVING?

Before beginning this chapter I checked my Bible concor dance for references concerning *to give*, *gift*, and *giving*. I was surprised at the quantity of them, and also that so many more references applied to God's gifts to us than ours to Him. I shouldn't have been surprised. God is a realist. He, of all persons, knows that the old cliche "It is impossible to outgive God" is true.

But there are passages of Scripture concerning our giving, and after studying most of them carefully, I've decided to consider two. The first is II Corinthians 9:7.

> Every man according as he purposeth in his heart, so let him give; not grudgingly, or of necessity: for God loveth a cheerful giver.

If you've attended church most of your life, you've heard

the hopeful minister or priest declare, "God loveth a cheer-ful giver," so often that you may not listen any longer when the words are spoken. If this has happened for you, you're miss ing a lot. Find a way to allow the phrase "God loveth a cheer ful giver" to have meaning for you. Read it in a fresh translation or paraphrase. I still prefer the music of the old-er translations, but now and then a new set of words does help. This may be one important instance where that is true. After all, God does love everyone—even the stingy, who give mainly under duress or the threat of embarrass-ment.

Try the Living Bible:

> Everyone must make up his own mind as to how much he should give. Don't force anyone to give more than he really wants to, for cheerful givers are the ones God prizes.

Everyone should make up his own mind as to how *much* he really *wants* to give. Perhaps the TV evangelists and the ministers and priests who beg from their pulpits should read II Corinthians 9:7 again. Still, money is needed. And as long as we do not consult our hearts before we give, as long as we check our bank balances first, the pulpit and TV persuasion will undoubtedly go on.

Your mail each day may contain as many pleas for mon-ey as mine. Almost every cause is one about which I care. After all, fund raisers buy lists from magazines and other charitable and political groups, so that if you give to liberal causes, you will receive pleas for liberal causes. If you have given in the past to conservative causes, your mail comes now from the White House or some other bastion of Con-

servatism. I sel dom receive a plea for money from a pol-
itician whose views I don't share. Now and then there is a
slipup, but not often. We are all bombarded with folders
and pamphlets bearing the heartbreaking faces of starving
children—stomachs distended, flies crawling in their eyes.
This is not propaganda. The pic tures are real. My own heart
has, by now, an old refrain: "If only I made enough money
to help them all!" I am besieged by pleas for money from
fine groups fighting to protect our fragile environment. I
belong to most of them, pay my dues regularly. Now that
the current administration poses such a threat to the prog-
ress we environmentalists have made through the years, I
long to give still more. I project twenty to thirty years in
the future and imagine what could happen to those who are
forced to live near our wildly dangerous nu clear plants and
waste dumps, and after I've given all I possi bly can, I have
real trouble throwing the environmental litera ture in the
wastebasket. Money is needed always for both Catholic and
Protestant missionary work. Money is needed to help protect the freedom of the press, the freedom of speech, to fight
censorship. Libraries, especially with Federal funds slashed,
are desperately in need, as are historical societies and pres-
ervation groups. The arts are suffering, too.

But wait. We are not, according to the Bible, to give ac
cording to the impact of the plea for assistance. I go back to
the King James version of what St. Paul wrote in his second
letter to the Corinthians: "Every man according as he purposeth in his *heart*, so let him give."

"Where your treasure is, there will your heart be also."
Who holds your heart? Where is it? Who holds my heart?

Do you ever consult with God before you give? Many
do, thank heaven. I do, not out of piety, but out of necessity,

and God has given us many guidelines. "Freely have you received, freely give." How good is God? "It is more blessed to give than to receive." When we try it, we know beyond doubt that those words are true. And yet we are urged to consult our own hearts. "As a man purposeth in his heart . . ." What does your heart tell you? Does it tell you to give to assuage even one small need *today* and leave your own future in God's hands?

Because of my sedentary life and my heredity, I am constantly overweight. Does my heart dare tell me to throw that plea from Food for the Hungry in the wastebasket?

I need only to pick up my long-ago book *The Burden Is Light* to be reminded that since my own turning to Christ, God has seemed to do nothing but give to me. How can I toss out a plea for money to buy Bibles for those who have never yet heard of Jesus Christ? In fact, I do glance now and then at *The Burden Is Light* for my own balance. The book has been in print for over a quarter of a century and I have been a follower of Jesus Christ for more than thirty years, but I never, never want to begin to allow that moment of turning to dim. I purpose in my heart not to forget for one moment that everything I have I have been *given*. When I make the slightest effort to keep that firmly in mind, I can then consult my heart and trust my instincts to give.

One of the most truly generous persons I've ever known is my beloved friend Anna B. Mow, who has never had enough material possessions to keep her awake for a single night. Now and then, when I can't think of the right gift in a pack age for her birthday or Christmas present, I send her a check. I know when I write it, make it out to Anna B. Mow, that it won't remain with Anna B. Mow for any longer than it takes her to get the proper money order to send it

to someone in India who "has trouble buying groceries."
That's fine with me, because I know Anna well enough to
know that as soon as she consults her great heart, my birthday check will take to the air toward India. "Everyone must
make up his own mind as to how much he should give."
And to whom.

When someone sends you a card at Christmas inform-
ing you that a gift has been given in your name to CARE
or to World Vision or Food for the Hungry or some other
organi zation geared to send help directly to those in need,
does it annoy you? It annoys some people. I've heard it said
that such giving is cheap. "It irks me when someone makes
a con tribution in my name and calls it a gift to me. After
all, the giver gets a contribution deduction on his income
tax, doesn't he?"

What if he does? Don't you care about the giver, too?

We all have tics and God knows that. He still *gave* Himself to us that day on His cross, tics and all. Sin and all.
When we examine our hearts before making a gift, what we
find isn't always comforting. Not for me, at least. I freely admit to some quick mental budgeting and God is not averse
to this. I don't think he loves a foolish giver in any special
way. He loves a *cheerful* giver. He isn't shocked or even surprised when I try to make up my mind about a certain gift,
that I also juggle in my mind the disappointing fact that if
I give the amount *needed*, I may have to cut short or forget about my longed-for vacation. For me to miss Atlanta
Braves spring training in West Palm Beach would be sac-
rificial giving. This doesn't startle God. He knows exactly
how much I look forward to it each year, how hard I work
to get my writing up to schedule so I can spare the time. He
knows even better than I how watching the balletic move-

ments of professional baseball players relaxes me.

The point of this discussion is that, although we are told to consult our heart, to make up our own minds, God already knows what's in both our hearts and minds. Even when I do my most concentrated consulting of my own heart, I don't see what He sees. I couldn't bear to. He can, thank heaven.

Do we give in order to please a demanding God?

I would hate to think I did that to Him—ever. If what He prizes is a cheerful giver. He must not prize a grudging giver. Test your heart for its cheerfulness while you write that check or take down that favorite extra coat from the closet. I know of no better way to come by guidance for giving. Testing your cheer gauge works every time.

The second Scripture to be considered is Matthew 25:40;

> . . . Verily I say unto you, Inasmuch as
> ye have done it unto one of the least of these my
> brethren, ye have done it unto me.

Here Jesus was speaking of His final judgment upon the quality of our lives, but He seldom spoke on just one level. Because He did become a human being. He used words—the human form of communication—but one reason why reading the Bible can seem always new is that behind His words lies the entire dimension of God.

Of course, "the least of these" means, among other things, kindness done for someone with no thought of praise. To give to what society labels an inconsequential person is not apt to bring much commendation.

I once heard a highly successful businessman say without a single blush or stammer: "I give heavily to the name evange lists on the TV and radio because they really show you their gratitude." And then he went on blithely to tell me of the marvelous golfing invitations and letters of commendation he had received from these "name" people for his generous gifts.

Well, no comment. None is needed. Jesus has already made the only necessary statement about that kind of giving: ". . . Inasmuch as ye have done it unto one of the least of these my brethren, ye have done it unto me."

An equally successful businesswoman wrote this: "I know we can't outgive God. I've gotten so I just sit back and wait for the extra business He's going to send me after I give to His work."

Again, no comment.

Jesus has spoken, enigmatically at times, of rewards. I've never dared allow myself to believe that He meant material rewards. He was not a material, earthly King. "The kingdom is within," He said ever so plainly. His disciples simply were as slow as we to learn and accept that His kingdom is a gift of the Spirit, therefore eternal. His gifts add to us at the very center of our being where the springs. Reward enough, to be sure, but not gifts with which we can buy a money market certificate that will earn us the highest possible rate of interest.

We are all susceptible to the promise of a reward. Cracker Jacks don't taste the way I remember them when I was a child, but I still buy them now and then at a ball game and the first thing I look for is the prize.

God knows this about us and so He saw to it that, if we re ally concentrate on what He said when He was on earth, our excuses for confusing spiritual with material rewards thin out and vanish.

Look at the answer He gave to His disciples, who, still un aware that the Kingdom about which He spoke was *not* of this world, asked: "Who is the greatest in the kingdom of heaven?"

I can't help but believe that He must have just looked at them for a long time before He answered. He had worked so hard to teach them what the Kingdom was about. He loved them so much. He knew that up to their human limitations, they also loved Him or they wouldn't have left their profes sions and families to follow Him. Jesus and these men had been together for a long time when they asked the question, "Who is the greatest in the kingdom of heaven?" And so He must have known deep disappointment at this proof that they, too, had missed His point. That they still looked for tan gible rewards and commendations.

In answer: "Jesus called a little child unto him and set him in the midst of them, and said, "Verily I say unto you, except ye be converted, and become as little children, ye shall not enter into the kingdom of heaven."

What does becoming a child mean?

To me it means a simplicity with God not at all charac teristic of a successful adult. The disciples wanted success. They wanted someone to be great among them. They wanted someone to have a "big name." To be famous. To be known.

Their master brought "one of the least of these" into the circle and quietly knocked all their misguided ambitions onto the scrap heap.

He not only told us that we give directly to Him when we give to one of the "least of these " He also said that we were to tell no one whatsoever about our contribution. Even He could not have made this plainer:...when thou doest thine alms, do not sound a trumpet before thee, as the hypocrites do in the synagogues and in the streets, that they may have glory of men. Verily I say unto you, They have their reward. But when thou givest alms, let not thy left hand know what thy right hand doeth: That thine alms may be in secret: and thy Father which seeth in secret himself shall reward thee openly."

Don't let your left hand know what your right hand is doing!

We've heard and read that for much of our lives, but have you thought about what it really means? Can anything be more hidden, more a secret, than that? And when He reminds us that *only* the Father sees in secret and rewards us openly in His way, we should begin to see that alms given in return for gratitude from the recipient, for that special golfing invitation, that personal letter written by that "big name," in no way matches what Jesus said.

As did His disciples following Him about the dusty roads of Judea, we miss the point. Jesus came bringing an inner kingdom. He came, the King of the inner kingdom. Our gifts may be hard, spendable cash gifts, but their motivations and rewards are to be *inner*. We are to give according to our hearts. If we can give cheerfully, if we can enjoy it, God will be especially glad in His Heart. I doubt that He thought up the idea of sending a "free book" or a "free cross that glows in the dark" as a reward for a five-dollar check. I don't condemn these incentive tokens offered by fund raisers, but I don't accept them. When and if I send a gift, I ask not to be sent anything. Is this splitting hairs? Perhaps. But I find Jesus' incentives to give far more compelling than any reward I could be sent via a computer.

Giving of time or money makes anyone feel better and

that is reward enough. That is, we feel better if we have been cheerful in the giving. Simply being cheerful causes us to feel well.

But enough of gimmicks and rewards and the desire to be recognized or praised or thanked. All of this falls to one side when we spend any time at all thinking about the Giver Himself.

"For God so loved the world . . ." Democrats and Republicans, Tories and Socialists, Catholics and Jews and Protestants, and Quakers and Unitarians, good people and bad, the selfish and the unselfish. "For God so loved the *world* that he *gave* his only begotten Son "

God so loved the world that He came Himself in the Person of Jesus of Nazareth—His Son—to get into our confusions and superficialities with us. He Himself *is* our salvation. I don't pretend to understand the gift of my salvation, but I go on trying to learn more and more of the Giver.

"Thanks be to God," Paul wrote, "for his unspeakable gift."

Giving matters. The spirit in which we give matters still more.

7

IS IT WHAT
WE ARE LIKE?

What are you like? What am I like?

Can we ever know fully on this earth? Or do we move through our days seeing ourselves "through a glass darkly"?

Does it really matter what we are like? Does it matter that we know ourselves? Mystery must be acknowledged when we concentrate on the things of God. If mystery and the need for faith in what we cannot prove are absent or ruled out in our thoughts, if we insist upon common sense only, we are almost stopped in our tracks. Still, even common sense will tell us that if both persons involved in a friendship lack self-knowledge, the friendship grows bumpy. I will be able to ad just to your personality quirks far more quickly if I also know my own. The reverse is, of course, true. You will adjust to me far more easily if you have some self-knowledge. Each one of us is urged to "know thyself."

But if we stop with self-analysis, no matter how plainly

we see, we can run headlong into trouble. Some time ago I wrote a book entitled *Leave Yourself Alone*. This was my straight forward response to the spate of self-analysis, self-help, and self-improvement books that have for years flooded the market. They sell, too. It isn't as much fun to leave our selves alone as it is to pamper and analyze and concentrate on improving ourselves.

It is said that we are part of what is called the Me Generation. Well, in the sense that fewer and fewer persons are willing to sacrifice themselves for their country, their princi ples, their neighbor's comfort, their fellowman's welfare, we are perhaps more self-absorbed than fifty years ago. When I was a child, a man or woman in trouble on the street for any reason was surrounded almost at once with other people offering help. Now people tend to pass by, to look the other way so as not to become involved. You've read this a hundred times in newspapers and magazines. You've heard and seen it on radio and TV. But I wonder if at the very core of human nature, we have changed all that much. I will be sixty-six as you read this. I watch myself like a hawk to avoid falling into the easy trap of believing that there really are such things as "good old days." It was a far simpler world when there were fewer people in it, but I've researched and written too many historical novels to believe for one minute that a majority of men and women have ever ultimately been motivated by unselfishness.

It is still popular for politicians to argue for "what is in the best interests of *our* country." They speak of their desire for peace in the world, but knowing that really won't motivate a voter, they are forced to add that this or that arms sale is in the best interest of *our own country—whatever* "best interest" may be.

You don't need to take my word for the fact that man's basic self-absorption has not changed much. Jesus lived on this earth almost two thousand years ago and He took great pains to teach that: "Except a corn of wheat fall into the ground and die, it abideth alone . . ." and that "He that loveth his life shall lose it."

One of Christ's most memorable stories is the story of the Good Samaritan. (Luke 10:30-36) Two men, religious profes sionals—a priest and a Levite—passed the wounded man by on the other side of the road. Only one Samaritan traveler crossed over to help. Our news accounts of the indifference of the Me Generation are not actually unique to our century or even to our decade.

Interest in ourselves is as old as the Garden. Self-knowledge is interesting to most of us. As a Christian I don't believe in astrology, but I read my horoscope when I happen to see it in print because I'm interested in almost anything about me. Even those among us who go on and on about our shyness are still going on about ourselves. When we run ourselves down, we are not only insulting the Creator God, we are being self-attentive. Self-knowledge is a good thing—a necessary thing if we are to live adequately, but without the simultaneous study of *God's nature*, it can twist us into painfully ingrown bores.

I wish there were a way to write the last four chapters of this book at once. I can't and so I must ask you to concentrate and move with me through them. Reader participation is always necessary. The author can do only his or her share of a book. For these remaining chapters your participation is required.

The title *What Really Matters* has directly to do with what is ultimately essential in an adequately lived Christian life. Each chapter is important. Each matters. But if I am successful at all, you will have long ago sensed a movement toward a final chapter. This chapter, does it matter *what we are like*? will lead into the next one; Does our commitment to Christ matter? That will lead into how much it matters that we know something of what He is really like, which in turn leads to the final chapter—His commitment to us.

So, does it matter what we ourselves are like? Of course it matters. But I find an easy danger here: It matters what *we* are *really* like, which is often not what we *think* we are like.

There is an enormous wave of right-wing politico-religious indignation sweeping across the United States right now. I will not attach any labels, but if you are battling your way along in the force of that wave—or if, as I am, you are horrified by it—I believe you will know what I mean. A group of religious leaders have taken judgment into their hands and have, while still mentioning Jesus Christ frequently in their sermons and TV lectures as though they have His endorsement, suddenly changed the things of the spirit to the things of politics.

My New Testament tells me that Jesus declared that Christians are to be known by their fruits. "By their fruits ye shall know them." I find no verse and chapter that says, "By their politics ye shall know them." Politics can be motivated by the things of the spirit, if we have a fairly clear view of what spirit is, but I will go to my grave believing that there are authentic, loving, caring Christians who also happen to be Democrats and Republicans. Which ticket they vote for at the polls is not the issue. Hearts are the issue.

The young Man on His Cross hung there with both arms stretched out toward the entire world. It bears repeating here: "For God so loved the *world* that he gave . . ." Anyone who hugs his own version of truth to himself and alienates those who may disagree on a few points shows no kinship to this young Man on His Cross. *God makes no hit lists.* Nor does He buy lists from others. God is neither liberal nor conservative. He is God. No one can ever convince me that He loves a Republican Congress more than He loves a Democratic Congress. "For God so loved the *world*...He loves each one of us—best. Only God could do that.

The Lord God doesn't have to buy lists of names so that He doesn't waste postage and computer printouts on those who disagree with Him. Every man and woman and child in the world is God's chosen. "I, if I be lifted up . . . will draw *all men* unto me."

His love. His drawing power, is all inclusive.

When we catch ourselves, for any reason—even the best reason—becoming exclusive, beware. Open-mindedness should be the Christian's principal goal. Jesus took pains to warn us that we simply *are not to judge* at all. St. Matthew makes it abundantly clear: "Judge not that ye be not judged." The words of Jesus Himself. Then, in verses 3, 4, and 5 of chapter 7, Matthew quotes the Lord in one of His most attention-grabbing illustrations:

And why beholdest thou the mote that
is in thy brothers eye, but considerest
not the beam that is in thine own eye? Or
how wilt thou say to thy brother. Let me pull
out the mote out of thine eye; and behold, a
beam is in thine own eye? Thou hypocrite,
first cast out the beam out of thine own eye;
and then thou shalt see clearly to cast out
the mote out of thy brother's eye.

My understanding of these strong words of Jesus is that under no circumstances am I to judge anyone. This does not mean that we grow soft and permissive. To claim that it does is superficial thinking, if it is thinking at all. To me it simply means that we are *not* to play God under any circumstances. Here again we can have our thinking clarified in no uncertain terms by Jesus Christ Himself: "For the Father judgeth no man, but hath committed all judgment unto the Son: That all men should honor the Son, even as they honor the Father."

It is not only an enormous relief to me that the Son will be my judge, it is unequivocal evidence that I certainly have no business trying it myself.

Certainly not to the wild extreme of deciding that someone is sinning should he disagree with me politically!

I received a letter the other day from an intense soul who is a contributing member of one of the right-wing politico-religious groups. This is what she wrote: "I do feel your books are fine. Certainly I enjoy reading them, but I feel I cannot go on in them until I know you are of a sound Christian political viewpoint." She then went on to ask my views on abortion, homosexuality, the Equal Rights Amendment, censorship of "dirty" books in public and school libraries, and on and on.

I doubt that she buys any more of my books. I answered her as carefully as I could. But I did not feel that she had any right to judge me on a single issue mentioned. That is the Son's right. I told her that her list of "test questions" for judging me was a simple confusion of apples and oranges. I don't write books on any single-issue questions. What I believe or don't believe politically is between God and me. Her letter wasn't very loving in tone, but I prayed for love for her. My prayer was answered to the extent that I now feel genuine concern for her and her crusading friends. If any reader of these pages has become disenchanted with me. I'll be sorry, but I still believe that God needs lovers, not fighters.

> For God so loved the world, that he
> gave his only begotten Son, that *whosoever*
> believeth in him should not perish, but have
> everlasting life. For God sent
> *not* his Son into the world *to condemn* the
> world; but that the world through him
> might be *saved*.

In all fairness to these well-meaning, embattled souls who mistrust me or anyone else because of our political persua sions, I wonder if they really know themselves. I wonder if they see themselves as condemning those whom they oppose. Is it enough to declare that we love the sinner but hate his or her sin? Shouldn't we practice love, too? Should we really go on confusing apples and oranges? True, Jesus told us that we were "the salt of the earth," "the light of the world," but He also told us plainly that we are not to judge or condemn, lest we be judged and condemned according to our own motives.

As long as we read our Bibles, attend church, pay our bills, assume our responsibilities, and pray—is that enough? Doesn't it matter what we are *like* in the process? I believe it does.

The night before they killed Jesus He went to great length to remind His disciples of what to Him must have seemed to be of prime importance:

> If ye abide in me, and my words abide

in you, ye shall ask what ye will, and it
shall be done unto you. Herein is my
Father glorified, that ye bear much fruit;
so shall ye be my disciples. As the
Father hath loved me, so have I loved
you: *continue ye in my love.*

Jesus spoke to His friends, His disciples, that night: And
He said something I dare not forget: "Continue ye in my
love." He did not say "Continue ye in my judgment."

This is my commandment, That ye love one
another, as I have loved you. Ye are my
friends, if ye do whatsoever I command you.

Just think of it! We can actually be the friends of God
Himself, if we do what He says to do. And "This is my com
mandment, That ye love one another, as I have loved you."

Is that possible? Is it possible for us to be like that?

Not on our own, certainly. I once read and still remember that "self-righteousness is the devil's masterpiece to
make us think well of ourselves." To me self-righteousness
is to believe we are right and that if anyone dares to disagree, he is wrong. Dwight L. Moody once said, "You can
always tell when a man is a great way from God when he
is always talking about himself, and about how good he is."

"Trust not in thine own righteousness." Our righteousness can too easily slip sideways into self-righteousness. But
is it possible to show only God's righteousness? Really to be
like Him?

I doubt that anyone but Jesus ever demonstrated that
wholly on this earth. But Christians are supposed to believe

that God has worked out a way for God Himself to go right on living His life in and through us by His Holy Spirit. That sounded only weird to me once. Now it is only practical.

Here again Jesus is speaking to His disciples on the night before the Crucifixion: . . I tell you the truth; It is expedient for you that I go away: for if I go not away, the Comforter will not come unto you; but if I depart, I will send him unto you. . . . . When He, the Spirit of Truth, is come, he will guide you into all truth."

Anyone who believes in Jesus Christ can, when he chooses, show the very righteousness of God. And if God did reveal Himself in Jesus Christ, His word is enough for me.

Then, what am I really like as a person and does it matter in the long run?

Well, I am certainly self-righteous in many areas of my life. I shouldn't be. I don't have to be but I am, so welcome me to the human race as I welcome you. Somehow I feel sure that if ever a man had to do battle with self-righteousness, it was Paul—surely before and undoubtedly after his conversion on the Damascus Road.

Paul was an intellectual, a highly educated and cultivated man. He was, I believe, a most opinionated man, too. His opinions before his encounter with the living Lord were so hot and so extreme that they sent him out to hunt down and kill those who did not follow his own religion—which meant, at that time, that he was out to kill Christians. Then Christ met and changed him. Still, it doesn't surprise me at all that it was the Christian Paul who wrote in his letter to the Ephesians: "And be renewed in the spirit of your mind." Neither does it surprise me that he repeated a similar admonition concerning the workings of our mind in his letter to the Philippians: "Let this mind be in you, which also was in Christ Jesus."

Opinions spring from our minds. Paul's brilliant mind kept him focused on the need to give the Spirit full sway. Our pet opinions, judgments, are precious to us. Sometimes we revel in expressing them and let the chips fall where they may. Liberals enjoy looking down on conservatives. Conservatives enjoy feeling superior to liberals. Protestants frequently feel that they have a better handle on the truth than Catholics and some Catholics feel that their grasp of the truth is absolute. We can go on with these judgments: one race against another, one system of government against another, even one sporting event against another. I love baseball and am bored to death all fall and winter while football is king. "I'm surprised that you like baseball," a friend said the other day. "It's such a plebeian sport." Well, if it is, then I'm a plebeian and proud of it. I tend to think football is plebeian!

What we are like as people is more often than not directly traceable to our prejudices and opinions. If they are allowed to swing wildly in all directions, we are just not very easy to be with. If a man or woman finds it easy to love his or her own opinions supremely, that person is generally hard to like. Some of this book is an outgrowth of what I began to see a long time ago during the writing of a book tided *The Wider Place*. I now see the Christian who knows himself fairly well as leaving a wide-open space for others. We are not their judge. God is. Once I have faced my own lacks, my own failings, my own sins, my own eccentricities, I well give you a wider place in which to discover yours. That is your work, not mine.

I read Thomas á Kempis soon after my own conver-

sion to Jesus Christ. One line I still think about: "An humble knowledge of thyself is a surer way to God than a deep
search after learning." Knowing ourselves as we are is humbling. Not defeating, humbling. We belong to the Victor. He
can handle our defeats if we let Him. But nothing makes us
so charitable, so forgiving of the faults of others, as to learn
our own.

Of course, it matters whether or not we are extreme by
nature. I tend to be. In retrospect I see no possibility that I
might have achieved even a measure of balance in my life
without a steady and growing knowledge of Christ, without
His life in me while I try to live mine in an adequate Christian way. It also matters whether we are shy or daring by
nature. You may be shy and cautious. You may not plunge
without first thinking for a long time. I'm a plunger. There is
no virtue involved either way, as I see it. Daring individuals
can leap quickly into an active faith in God. Cautious folk
like Jesus' disciple Thomas need time to think. They need
time before they jump but then they usually don't turn back.
It matters, too, if we've been loved as children growing up
in a secure home. I have never wondered about being loved.
My parents gave me no reason to wonder. As a result I had
no problem at all—once I realized that there was a God—in
believing that He loved me. If you do have trouble believing
that He loves you as you are, be patient with yourself. He
will never withdraw His love.

What matters where our human natures are concerned
is the intention of our *hearts* toward Him. What matters
to God is the *state of our hearts*. I know certain Christian
groups which keep smiling all the time, believing that is a
sign of "spirituality." Well, Christians *can* smile at what may
make others weep. The joy of God is indestructible. We may

not always *feel* joyful. Feelings are like clouds, they change. God's joy remains. Smiling and looking peaceful should be one characteristic of His followers, but His followers are human, too. God pays little attention to the way we look. He stays aware of our hearts.

In I Samuel, chapter 16, you can find an apt illustration of God's attentiveness to our attitude of heart. Samuel, in some grief and trembling, could not quite believe that the Lord had really chosen him. Another man named Eliab *looked* far more like God's anointed. This is what happened: "And it came to pass, when they were come, that he looked on Eliab, and said. Surely the Lord's anointed is before him. But the Lord said unto Samuel, Look not on his countenance, or on the height of his stature; because I have refused him: for the Lord seeth not as man seeth; for man looketh on the outward appear ance, but the Lord *looketh* on the heart."

The italics again are mine. It is so important that we remember that it is what we are like inside that matters to God. Inside, where only He can see, where only He can bear to see.

8

IS IT WHAT
HE IS LIKE?

Deep-thinking, educated minds for centuries have explained man's need for religious belief this way: If there were no God, we would have to invent one.

A few days ago I listened carefully for an hour to one of the twentieth century's most brilliant scientists as he spoke with contagious enthusiasm of his work and his life. The man was Dr. Jonas Salk, who discovered a vaccine which has, as he said, "taken away the fear" from millions.

When I was a child, polio haunted parents constantly. I, along with all other children, could have fallen victim to it at any time. Polio crippled bodies. It even killed. I was fortunate. Thousands of people my age today still breathe by lung machines or swing their bodies along on steel crutches because of it. Dr. Salk's vaccine has been used so successfully that most people have forgotten polio.

Oh, we remember it when we remember President

Franklin D. Roosevelt but not having at that time the massive news coverage we have now, we seldom saw him swing along on his crutches. He stood tall and exuded strength for a whole country but he was a victim of polio, too. Mothers went from door to door once a year collecting for the March of Dimes to fund polio research. Their efforts paid off. I heard Dr. Salk say that they did. That money enabled him to make his shining discovery.

I haven't been so stimulated or informed by a TV interview in a long time. I hung on every word. He is a quiet, certain, far-seeing, thoughtful man. A philosopher as well as one of our most brilliant scientists. When the interviewer, John Callahan, asked his usual probing question about Jonas Salk's faith, the great man, with genuine humility, attempted to articulate it. His faith evidently lies in the order of the universe, in the vast, still untapped potential of the human mind. He is what some Christians rail against as a humanist. Isn't it a paradox that some Christians need more humanity than they seem to possess? Dr. Salk's life is a bright path of contribution to his fellow beings.

Only last night, as I discussed this chapter with my good friend the Reverend Dr. Junius Martin he reminded me that the beloved Scottish theologian John Bailie had said in effect that a person can believe in God with the top of his mind, while he denies God from the bottom of his heart. Bailie believed that the reverse is also true: A person can believe in God from the bottom of his heart, while denying Him with the top of his mind. Jesus went even farther. In Mark 9:40 He declares that ". . . he that is not against us is on our: part." More clearly here the Living Bible reads: "Anyone who isn't against us is for us."

I heard no word of condemnation from Dr. Jonas Salk

toward those of us who believe that God has revealed Himself in Christ. I thought a long time about Dr. Salk as a person that night after the interview ended—in neither a worshipful nor a condemnatory way. Who am I to condemn a man or a woman who does not see God as I see Him? Jesus came "not to condemn the world, but that the world through him might be saved."

I neither have time nor energy nor wisdom for condemnation. As I grow older, I do find myself wanting honestly to understand those who don't agree with me. I wish I could ask Jonas Salk about his lonely moments, his times of grief, his disappointments and failures. I doubt that anyone who ever lived never failed in some area. Every adult experiences sor row and heartbreak. I'm also certain that no virtue is involved in my caring about the heart of a successful, famous man like Dr. Salk when his dark times come. I simply believe that we all share some basic human helplessness and I am curious to know how such helplessness is handled without some under standing, some idea, of what God's intentions toward us are in our helplessness.

Can the human potential and the orderly universe heal broken hearts?

At no time in my own life have I been considered brilliant or highly successful, but I did live thirty-three years without any firm idea of God beyond the quickly discarded, somewhat sentimental, secondhand Sunday School concept that comes easily to most children. From the ages of fourteen to thirty- three I entered actively into religious discussions on the side of those who condescend to say: "All right, if you feel weak enough to think you need some sort of god, fine. Not me."

I can still hear myself make what was probably a faulty

philosophical sweep through the ages of man following a sophomore course in the history of religion, in which I de clared that the ancients, because they were not yet "ad vanced" in science, "created a god behind every bush." I even went so far as to agree that they needed their gods. They were simple, ignorant folk who thought very little for them selves and so on and on ad nauseam. I can laugh at myself for much of that specious argument now, especially because it hadn't dawned on me that the ancient Greeks and Romans were—are, to this day—more advanced than we in many of their human concepts. Mainly, I can laugh (or want to weep) at myself because of my own intellectual dishonesty. I was young, true, but young people experience heartbreak and fail ure and disappointment, too. My needs then, in proportion to my needs now, were just as great. I simply didn't have any idea of what God—if it turned out that there was a God—was like, and so I discarded Him.

Didn't I have religious training? Of course I did. Some of my young friends who attended A e same church services and Sunday-school classes with me evidently became believers then and are still believers today. There is no answer for me other than the fact that I didn't have any concept of my own on which I could fasten anything resembling faith. I heard and read all the Bible stories. Jesus Christ's name was as familiar as my brother's name to me. Still, with no conflict whatever, in my middle teens, I came to the conclusion that He was one of the world's great teachers, to be revered and spoken of as one revered Socrates and Plato. This probably sounded terribly intellectual to my unformed mind.

Except for Mother I had known no Christians who struck me as particularly literate or perceptive or much different from the remainder of the human race. And so, I suppose I simply accepted that Mother was unique anyway and let it go at that. I had been exposed at church to lots of Christians who seemed to spend their energies on prohibitions. Don't do this, don't do that. They repeated the familiar phrases about salvation and conversion and how sinful young people needed to straighten up and please God, or else. By nature I am not a conformist. I'm still not, although I've gained enough emotional maturity to know that I no longer find it amusing to shock people. In fact I now find it rather childish. I'm sure my present life wouldn't pass muster with many of those dear, rigid souls at the church where I grew up, but they no longer represent God to me. No one represents God to me but God Himself, and therein lies the freedom He promised.

In my early years I tried to please my mother and father because I loved them and I knew they loved me. When I left home for the university at barely sixteen, I still tried to please them with my grades and the tone of my letters home, but as was normal, I began first of all to please myself. I can still see my heavily underlined comment on my university registration card:

Do not invite me to church. I don't attend church.

To me that was an exhilarating declaration of independence. I had attended church all through my childhood and now I had "put off childish things." There is nothing at all extraordinary about this little story. I was born with an inquiring mind, an insatiable love of literature, of music, of art— and mainly, of writing. I had no need of religion.

About that time there was one of those typical church fights among the flock with whom I grew up. My mother, caught in the middle of it, tried to make peace and found her self outnumbered. In total disgust I informed her that she was wasting her time with those people. The civil war within God's house delighted me. It was my final reason for declar ing my own freedom from such "ignorance" forever.

I entered my twenties, living my own life, and trying to break into radio writing in Chicago, financially supported by my parents. I reveled in my "liberty," but I suffered heart aches, failures, and disappointments. In short, life began to happen to me as it does to us all. So far as I remember now, I gave no thought to the possibility that if I believed in some thing higher than the top of my own head, I might lead a more adequate life. Church never crossed my mind, except once when I attended my ultrareligious grandmother's fu neral. I had some writing success, many friends, loved big-city life, and went bumbling on in my chosen way until I en tered my thirties. And then, after a separation of eighteen years, I saw again a high-school friend whom I had always considered as "much in the know" as I, and got the shock of my life.

She was a Christian!

I thought—'What a pity, with her brain and talent."

Details of this story are told in my book *The Burden Is Light*. Within a few weeks after our time together I, too, was a believer in Jesus Christ. In my usual extreme fashion, I plunged into the life of faith. I was poor for the first time, but lyrical over my discovery. I hated the thought of wasting time in sleep, as I'd always hated it, but for a totally different reason: I was joyfully blinded by Christ Himself and could scarcely wait to wake up each day   because there were all those books to read in which I could find out more and more of what *He is really like*.

This is not a retelling of how my conversion happened.

It is the telling of why it happened. Those who have read my older books know that I am a Christian for one reason and one only: I became convinced through that childhood friend that God has not hidden Himself from us. He has not kept His true nature a secret from anyone. All we need know of God is available to us. All we have the capacity to know of His intentions toward us, we can discover when we set ourselves to learn of Jesus Christ.

The Scriptures on this point are endless: "If you have seen me, you have seen the Father. I and the Father are one." Jesus said that of Himself. He also said: "No man cometh to the Father but by me." What did He mean by that? Was He setting up a roadblock for those who do not believe that God revealed Himself in Jesus of Nazareth? No. As I understand that verse now, after thirty-three years as His follower, I believe that Jesus was saying simply that God is God, but there is no other way for you to begin to grasp His true nature except by following His Son. By learning of Him. "Learn of me." Jesus said that, too. It is the key to finding out how it is that His yoke can be easy. His burden light. His actual statement bears repeating here. It is found at the end of the eleventh chapter of St. Matthew:

> Come unto me, all ye that labour and are
> heavy laden, and I will give you rest.
> Take my yoke upon you, and learn of me;
> for I am meek and lowly in heart: and ye
> shall find rest unto your souls. For my
> yoke is easy, and my burden is light.

We usually concentrate on finding the "rest" and allowing Him to share the yoke and the burden with us. But again, the key to being willing to trust Him to do this is to *learn of him*. I've written already that faith is almost the automatic result of finding out what He is really like. If we know someone to be trustworthy, trust comes. If we know someone to be tricky and fickle, we doubt.

The writing of this book has been a most meaningful and enlightening time for me, having reached the age when I can say that I have followed Christ for half of my life on earth. I have no authority as a Bible teacher, but I do have authority as someone who tried life without God for as long as she has tried life with Him. The difference is startling. It continues to startle me, I simply do not forget what it was like under that low ceiling—on my own. I simply do not forget the emptiness of the moments before sleep at night when I punched and pounded my pillow trying to ratio-nalize my problems away, trying vainly to remind myself that even troubles do end, but longing for someone to tell who could help me. I just do not forget how tiring it was to swagger, to pretend life was going along just fine. Of course, I don't forget how desperately afraid I was that I would run out of something to write. Writing had already become my reason for getting up in the morning, but with no conscious contact with the Creator, it is no wonder I was anxious. I worked hard then, too, but in retrospect contrasting that time with this—I worked in a vacuum.

I had no polestar.

I have had a polestar since the autumn of 1949. And my polestar is not a theory; not a principle; not a dogma; not an organized church. My polestar is a Person. Certainly I don't know all there is to know about Him. But I am learning dai-ly, as anyone who makes that initial leap of faith can learn.

Back in the first chapter of this book you read that there *moved* into my consciousness the firm conviction that, indeed, God would be discoverable to me if I dared to get acquainted with Jesus Christ. I had felt so lost and suddenly I was not lost anymore. Nor was I alone. And dumbfounded, I came to see that in my early years I had blamed Christianity for the prickly dispositions, the self-righteous- ness, the heavy-handedness of some of those church people. We dare not count on any human being to reveal God for us. "No man hath seen the Father at any time. The only begotten Son, he hath declared him."

Just as we dare not allow even the most lovable saint to give us our concept of God, we dare not trust our own perceptions in deciding about the caliber of someone else's faith. No one on earth is totally like Jesus Christ. No one has "made it" to Christ-likeness. Many strongly and blessedly resemble Him, but we are told that we wont be "like him" until we "are with him." Many persons talk a lot about their faith. Some do this from habit or because they consider it "witnessing." Others do it from sincere, overflowing hearts. Talk is not the point. *He* is the point. The most surprising people have written some startling truths about Him. Read the following quotation and try to guess its author:

> The nature of Christ's existence is mysterious,
> I admit; but this mystery meets the wants of man. . .
> Reject it and the world is an inexplicable riddle;
> believe it, and the history of our race is
> satisfactorily explained.

Are those the words of one of the world's great Christian philosophers? A known man or woman of God? What some would call a "saint"? No. The ambitious little French general with the famous forelock wrote it—Napoleon Bonaparte.

This Jesus Christ has a way of penetrating the most unexpected minds. He has a way of turning up in the least expected places. Christ bears no labels. Most of His followers do wear labels. We call ourselves liberal or conservative Christians. We call ourselves liturgical or Pentecostal Christians. Now it is popular to link the strange bedfellows of faith and politics. All beside the point. All in the final analysis irrelevant.

There isn't a man or woman on earth who can truly fudge the faith of anyone else. Oh, there are some whose faith has gone far enough to make them lovable, so that we easily believe they are Christians. But there are other Christians who seem to feel so superior to the rest of us that we tend to be puzzled. As Jesus said, "Ye shut up the kingdom of heaven against men." Either way, be it someone else's faith or lack of same, it is not our business to decide, if their semantics happen not to match ours. Or should they differ from us in lifestyle or politics.

I listen to certain TV sermons and read religious articles and books and find myself wondering what kind of God these people follow. He doesn't seem to resemble the God I follow except that we both call Him "Jesus Christ." Well, He can tolerate that. He is God. And the more we find out about His true nature, the less time we feel we need to spend judging or even wondering about anyone else.

I have never worried about the fact that I don't "witness" enough, because I've never understood how any of His followers could help mentioning a name as exciting, as all absorbing, as the name of Jesus Christ.

A troubled but honest man wrote to me, "I guess I'm

embarrassed to mention that I'm a Christian."

Interesting. But that could only be true *if* that embarrassed person has not yet found out about God's true nature. I agree wholly that the busybody believer who rushes about, Bible in hand, trying to force his or her theology down someone's throat, must be a driven extrovert at best. But, that isn't necessarily "witnessing" to *Jesus Christ* as He is. No need to force it. Good news is hard to keep to ourselves. Learn of Him and then be your natural self.

This inquiring, curious mind of mine hasn't even scratched the surface of knowledge about God yet and still He holds my attention hour after hour. It is still as magnetic a thing to me after more than thirty years to sit and marvel that Almighty God, seeing that we were not catching on to His true nature, thought to send Jesus so that all doubts could stop. "If you have seen me, you have seen the Father."

It is as simple as that.

John, known as "the beloved disciple," the young man who knew Jesus perhaps better than anyone else, is the Gospel writer who carefully and plainly lets us know that it is Jesus "who hath declared him" (the Father). John was so sure of this because he had been with his Master long enough to get to know Him *as He is*. The same simple way is open to us. To all of us. Christ Himself made the Great Simplification when He said: "Learn of me." That is the secret. That is the shining secret.

I took the initial leap of faith on the sudden realization that even I could get to know God—not as some vague distant Deity making celestial demands impossible for me to meet, but as a Person who had already given me Himself. Even His hideous execution acquaints me with Him. Over and over again I have written that the Man-God "died with

His arms stretched out to the whole world." He did not die clutching His own holiness to Himself. He died, arms out, shouting in effect: "I love you. I love you. This is what I'm really like!"

Jesus Christ, the Son of God, did not come to earth and die *only* in order to fulfill a long-ago prophecy. The prophecy is there because God knew we would not discover His real nature by any other means.

I can walk hospital corridors with the Man-God, Jesus Christ. I can talk to Him about weaknesses of my own too hu miliating to tell another human being. He knows about them anyway. I am free to tell Him, but I actually don't need to. I can sit down at this typewriter when my heart is breaking with grief or when I don't feel well and know that once I try, His creation will continue. I am, because of my confidence in the Man-God, because of what I've managed to learn of Him, no longer struggling to make contact. He has come to me as He has come to you. No one has to seek God. We need only to welcome Him. To thank Him for coming.

Rigid, doctrinaire believers who seem to confuse grace with morals have accused me and others of following a senti mental, do-gooder, soft God of love. The only times Jesus vented spleen at anyone in the entire New Testament account was toward the rigid, religious *t*-crossers and *i*-dotters whom He called "whited sepulchres," "hypocrites," and those who tried to make money in the Temple. These critical Christians who label me as too liberal and more centered on God's love than on His judgment have not seen my marked-up Bible.

His judgment is as much a part of His nature as His love. But, again, I am grateful that the Father "hath committed all judgment to the Son." Christ's judgment is the judgment of

God, not of human justice. If any one of us was to be judged spiritually by the best human judge in history, we would be doomed. Human judgment forces us to pay for our wrong-doings. God has already paid. Human judges sentence men to be killed. God's judgment touches the life which the human judge may destroy—and redeems it. When a life has been redeemed, it is then ready to be used.

I am corresponding these days with a comparatively young woman on Georgia's death row. I ache inside every time I write to her. Desperately I try to put myself in her place. I can't. Forcing any human being to sit in a cell and wait for months and years with only recrimination and dread and fear as companions is, to me, the cruelest punishment of all. But God has redeemed her. At times she seems almost cheerful. She doesn't try to hide her longing for freedom, but Christ has somehow freed her spirit. Whatever her wrongdoing, He has forgiven her. And in return for that forgiveness, that re demption, He hopes only for her love.

The God we follow in Jesus Christ is not a God of ven geance. He is the God of the turned cheek, the second mile, the outstretched arms.

The demanding God of punishment and vengeance often described by some devoutly religious leaders draws no one except through fear. Again, Jesus clarifies: "I, if I be lifted up from the earth, will draw all men unto me." Will draw, not terrify.

He was lifted up from the earth on a rough wooden cross. And from that cross, arms stretched wide. He prayed for those who had nailed Him there: "Father forgive them, for they know not what they do."

At the moment He prayed that prayer. He was allowing His heart to be tom open for all the world to see. For all the world to find out that this indeed is what Almighty God is really like.

> No man hath seen God at any time;
> the only begotten Son, which is in
> the bosom of the Father,
> *he hath declared him.*

9

IS IT OUR COMMITMENT TO HIM?

As soon as I decided to include this chapter on the importance of our commitment to Him, the old song based on the passage found in II Timothy 1 : 12 began running through my mind. Its melody isn't great music, and in order to make the rhythm of the words match the rhythm of the tune, one has to accent the last syllable of the word "believed" so that it is sung: believed. The refrain goes like this:

> For I know whom I have believed, and am
> persuaded that he is able to keep that which
> I've committed unto him against that day.

In the early months of my Christian life the song had special, deep meaning for me. After having lived by my own dictates and in a most opinionated way, I had begun an entirely new and unfamiliar way of life. The outward changes were far less traumatic for me than the inward. My whole viewpoint had been turned completely around. As thoroughly as I knew how, I had committed myself to Jesus Christ. I now know that I was extreme, in part because that is my nature, in part because some of my youthful impressions of Christianity were more rigid than I have found God Himself to be. But I knew that what really mattered for me at that point was to begin to the best of my limited knowledge of Him to see and act *from His viewpoint*, and not mine. So that when I was in church (unfamiliar surroundings, to say the least) and "I Know Whom I Have Believed" was sung, I sang lustily. I needed constant reminding that I was no longer the master. And when I sang that "he is able to keep that which I've com mitted. . . my will seemed to move still closer to His and I experienced enormous relief.

Why did I experience relief? Why do I still experience it?

The principal answer will be found in the final chapter when we look at what to me, in this stage in my Christian life, *really matters*. In evaluating the importance of our commitment to God in this chapter, the relief comes when we know that we have truly committed our *wills* and not merely our hopes or emotions.

We do have a part.

As with human friendship, genuine friendship with God means that there must be activity and response from both sides. His response, His activity in our behalf, is a certainty. A *fact*. The delightful Quaker writer Hannah Whitall Smith insisted that the fact of God precedes our faith in importance. And that what we call feeling pulls up a poor third. Fact, faith in the fact of Christ, and then feeling.

Several times a month I receive letters which read like this: "I committed my life to God, but most of the time I don't *feel* as though I did. One day I'm on cloud nine and the next day I 'm back thinking and acting in the old ways. How does this square with the claim that God doesn't change?"

It squares quite easily. Consult a dictionary. Commitment means: (1) the act of doing or performing something; and (2) the act of committing to the charge, keeping, or trust. In other words, true commitment requires a definite act of our *will*. Some of us seem not to have very strong or dependable wills and my guess is that we simply don't give them much exercise. I sit too much and so I am not a good long-distance walker. I bang on a manual typewriter for several hours each day and so I can peel potatoes or grate cheese as long as there are potatoes to be peeled and cheese to grate. My fingers are strong and well exercised.

It just so happens that my initial commitment to God in volved what must have been my total will. I wasn't sure of it then. I wouldn't know how to judge my will much more accu rately now. There is no virtue involved, but I do happen to be someone who isn't timid about risks. As a child, when I was learning to dive, I simply went out to the end of the diving board and plunged. The time required to commit our wills fully is not what matters ultimately. What matters is the extent of the commitment. Only you and God know how you fare here. Only God and I know as far as the matter of my will is concerned. When we think we've committed our wills and find out differently, that's all right. God will be waiting and He is unbelievably patient with us.

There *is* such a thing, you know, as settling an issue once and for all, and there *is* enormous relief in the act. To settle any commitment does not in any way mean that there won't be difficulties ahead. "In this world ye shall have tribulation." Jesus warned us about that, so trouble usually does come, but it shouldn't really surprise us. No one is immune to trouble.

There are schools of religious thought which seem to promise only joy and positive results up ahead. There can be more joy with God and there can, of course, be far more positive results. But in the New Testament there is no guarantee that joy and positive results will exclude the negatives of this life. Oh, Jesus did declare that He came so that we "shall have life and have it more abundantly," but He was too much of a realist to imply that there would not be rough patches. He came to offer us His redemptive power and love. That power and that love can strengthen and enlarge our capacities so that we will indeed experience "a more abundant life." If life were all sunshine and flowers to smell, we'd be bored in no time.

And perhaps these false expectations of only roses and moonlight cause some of us to question our own commitment to Him when there is no connection at all.

I did not become a believer in Jesus Christ, I did not, by an act of my will, enter into the eternal life he offers *expecting* ever to change my mind and hurry back to being my old self where everything was, at least, familiar. Oh, I thought of it a hundred times during the first year or so, but I didn't *entertain* the thought of running back. I didn't want life without Him ever again. The friend through whom I met Him had simply made it clear at the outset that the transaction—wordless though it was with me—was an eternal transaction. If I couldn't make it on that basis, she urged me not to enter in at all. That settled it for me.

We can, if we are even reasonably normal, truly settle a thing. Doing so isn't always easy. In fact, it is often extremely difficult, but *settling is possible.*

I'm sure some of you may have read this story in an older book of mine, or perhaps you have heard me tell it. It is one of my favorites and I can think of no other so appropriate here. In an earlier chapter I have written of my beloved friend Dr. Anna B. Mow. One day a number of years ago it so happened that she was speaking in a town only fifty miles from where I was also engaged. She had a free day and some one drove her to my motel. We hadn't been together in a cou ple of years, but as always, Anna was no sooner propped up on my bed, shoes off, feet up, then we were talking excitedly about ideas and newly learned truths. There is more than twenty years difference in our ages, but we've never noticed.

"I learned something this morning before they drove me here," Anna began, "from reading in the paper about that poor child Marilyn Monroe, who just had another divorce. My heart goes out to her! She seems so lost and confused. And—it came to me that I could learn more about commitment. You see, the difference between Marilyn Monroe and me is this— *I'm committed to Baxter Mow!*"

Anna was probably about seventy then, it was her day off, she wore no girdle, she wasn't dressed up, but suddenly I saw that she had hit upon what was truly the *main difference* be tween her and Marilyn Monroe, between her and many per sons who had never known the freedom of a true commit ment. "I am committed to Baxter!"

Anna is committed to Baxter, and after what is now more than sixty years of married life, that commitment hasn't wavered. Anna and Baxter are as different as a husband and wife can be. As she says, "I always want to get everything done yesterday and Baxter wants to get it done week after next." This hasn't affected the commitment one iota.

Churches—Protestant and Catholic—require some

kind of commitment to faith in Christ upon one's joining the church or becoming a communicant. Of course, there are as many degrees of involved will in these millions of commitments made in the past two thousand years as there have been persons making them.

In a restaurant the other night, from the booth behind where I sat, I heard a man say: "My wife and I joined the church last Sunday. Should have done it a long time ago. I've met lots of new people there. Good for business, along with being good for my soul."

An honest statement about one kind of commitment. "God is such a part of my life now that I wonder how I managed all those years without Him."

Another honest statement about another, seemingly deeper, commitment.

But wait . . . we make dangerous generalizations when we decide the nature of someone else's commitment to God. Certain religious groups set up rigid guidelines—literal regulations—about what constitutes genuine commitment. It took me some time to understand that in spite of the fact that David danced for joy in the Lord, these dear folk considered dancing a sin. In the tobacco-growing states I find far less "spiritual" condemnation of someone who happens to smoke. As we have already mentioned, other groups equate so-called Americanism with their brand of religion. I have been criticized for lack of commitment because I don't always indicate verse and chapter when I quote from the Bible in a book I happen to be writing. If I choose to keep the sentence smooth by integrating a phrase from the Scriptures into a sentence, avoiding the use of references, then I'm somehow suspect. Well, that's all right. God knows the extent of our commitment to Him and so do we. No one else needs to decide.

My mother was not a perfect woman, but thank God, neither was she a judging Christian. She and I agreed on the one Basic, Jesus Christ Himself, and beyond that we listened to each other and found our differing emphases interesting. Once she asked me: "Just what are these church people so angry about?"

If it didn't always give her the comfort it gives me that my late brother and father are together now with God, her nearly lifelong commitment to Christ was not in question. Her relationship to both loved ones was different from mine. Because I am no longer an out-and-out ascetic, as I was in the early days of my faith when I even stopped drinking coffee, to her my commitment was not in question.

Commitment—authentic commitment to God—changes us at the wellsprings of our being. Most of all it involves us there. And as nearly as I can understand, the wellsprings of our being controls our *attitudes of heart*.

Wasn't Jesus called a "glutton and a winebibber" by his religious critics? Wasn't He slandered because of the company He kept? But was His commitment to the Father really in question?

Dr. Billy Graham was roundly criticized many years ago for spending time with a well-known gangster. I don't know Billy Graham well, but I do know him, and only a superficial busybody would condemn him for this. The underworld figure had asked to see him obviously to find out about the God Dr. Graham follows. You may not agree with everything he preaches, but no one could honestly doubt Billy Graham's commitment.

I was interviewed yesterday for an hour. One of the ques tions asked went something like this: "What is your response to the criticism of many Christians that you have turned into such a recluse? You keep a lock on your gate, you have an un listed telephone, and you're very hard to see. What do you say to this criticism and what do you do with your time?"

My first reaction was to laugh a little. And then I said, 'Well, I know I'm criticized for being a recluse, but I didn't know so many of my Christian friends were in on it. First of all, I am still a working author and I have no apologies to make. My friend, the Atlanta writer Celestine Sibley, once wrote a newspaper column in which she wondered rather pointedly why people feel they can 'visit awhile' with a writer, who works full-time every day, more plausibly than they can wander into a classroom and visit with the teacher or knock on the door of an operating room for a word with the surgeon? Writing may not be as important as teaching or surgery, but it is work. Come what may, I write every day in the week. In order to keep the well filled, I must also study and read. I read through most evenings or listen to music or to games during baseball season. I have lots and lots of personal friends and I see them whenever possible. I live in a resort area and some days I am sure everyone in the world is on vacation but me. I am learning to be willing to be misunderstood. I do the best I can and that's it."

After the interview we discussed the question a bit. Part of the dissatisfaction, I learned, stems from the fact that I write historical novels along with books such as this one about liv ing. "Some Christians feel your commitment has lessened."

What are the results in our lives of genuine commitment to God?

They are too many for one chapter. But try this: To whom do you turn first—not after the shock has lessened—but first, when you learn tragic news? Unbroken commitment becomes a habit. The good, constructive kind of habit for which God created our minds. One of my dearest friends heard from the hospital that her husband was dead. Her first impulse, not act, but impulse, was to say: "Oh, Lord God, did You hear that? You've got to handle it for me! I can't."

That is a fruit of commitment—a lifetime of it. Then she gave way to her grief. Her husband was all she had on earth. But first she spoke to God directly—before she hung up the telephone.

In the next and final chapter we will look straight at His side of commitment. Of course, my friend whose husband had just died was sure of God. At a time Like that we don't have time to renew our faith. There isn't time to get out the Bible and hunt a verse. We have to have been an active participant in the friendship with the God who, from the beginning, has taken full responsibility for us.

I certainly don't condemn those who are not aware that He has done this from the beginning. I remember too well what it's like not knowing. But anyone can become aware.

Commitment is never, never to be measured only by outward appearance or church attendance or generosity or service. Commitment can be far more truly measured by attitude of heart in the tight, ugly, difficult places. In the case of my friend whose husband had just died in the hospital, there was some cause to think that an error in treatment had been made. The surgery on his esophagus was successful, but the cobalt, given later, burned up his lungs. My friend, his widow, said only: "Those doctors did their best. They loved him, too."

Would she have hurt anyone but herself had she not been so deeply committed to a forgiving God?

Some members of the so-called Christian Establishment—not all, some—tend to measure commitment by outward signs. I don't believe Jesus did and I base that belief on the marvelous story told by Matthew in chapter 26. Jesus was at dinner with his disciples in the home of a social outcast—Simon, the leper. "There came unto him a woman having an alabaster box of very precious ointment, and poured it on his head, as he sat at meat. But when his disciples saw it, they had indignation, saying. To what purpose is this waste? For this ointment might have been sold for much, and given to the poor. When Jesus understood it, he said unto them. Why trouble ye the woman? for she hath wrought a good work upon me."

Were Jesus' own disciples part of the religious Establishment? Bless them, they were still half in and half out. They were following Him. But like many of us, they didn't have it all straight about *who He really was*. Perhaps their needs had not yet surfaced enough for them to understand. The woman—not a "nice woman"—apparently did understand. No one knows her thoughts, or why she understood, but she did come and she did make what to Jesus was the supreme symbol of her commitment—not to the poor or to service or to generosity or to Bible study or to prayer or to the organized church—but to *Him*.

Only she and Jesus Christ knew the extent of her commitment. What the well-meaning disciples said was good, but to Jesus their so-called goodness lacked commitment. It *sounded* good. Society would have accepted and applauded giving to the poor. The woman with the alabaster box cared that night that only her Master knew.

Like her, countless people through the two thousand years since Jesus first said, "Follow me," have committed them selves, however haltingly. There simply is no following with out commitment to the One we follow. To follow means *to follow*. It doesn't mean to sit and rest when you feel like it, or to turn aside to handle a worthy project, or to be pleasing those who might criticize. It does not mean to pacify or appease. It means—*to follow*. And if we follow, there must be someone up ahead to lead.

> . . . when he putteth forth his own sheep,
> he goeth before them, and the sheep follow
> him; for they know his voice.

Does any of this mean that we cannot break our commitment and still return to following Him again at some future time? No. "He is the good shepherd." He keeps count. He keeps check. He misses one ordinary sheep immediately. He knows each name. "He calleth his own sheep by name," hunts until He finds the lost ones, and once more, "he leadeth them out."

10

WHAT REALLY MATTERS IS HIS COMMITMENT TO US

In each preceding chapter I have attempted to set down nine vital areas of living in conscious contact with the Re deemer God as He can be discovered in Jesus Christ. Each chapter is an important, integral part of that life: faith, prayer, growth, praise, service (friendship with Him), giving, what we are like, what He is like, our commitment to Him. All of these matter.

Through the half of my own earthly life lived with Him, all have come to be characteristics of the Christian walk. No one, certainly not I, has flawless faith, a perfect prayer life, or uninterrupted growth. I have yet to meet anyone who is a perfect friend to God, whose service glorifies Him in every way. I have yet to meet a totally selfless, generous giver; I have yet to meet anyone who is every moment Christlike; and, although I can speak only for myself where commitment to Him is concerned, mine is permanent, still far from perfect. These first nine chapters encompass the basics for us all—the basic, recognizable characteristics of what Paul called "the life hid with Christ."

But aren't they just that? Aren't they characteristics? Are they collectively or separately what makes for fruitful lives as Christians? Aren't they results of something else which mat ters ultimately?

Could we put it this way: All matter, but *what really mat ters*?

What makes it all happen?

As you read chapter 1 on faith, did you perhaps think with some misgivings about the quality of your faith? Did you cringe a bit at times because your faith seemed weak and ineffectual? As I see it, that is a wasteful thing for any of us to do. After having met and talked or corresponded with thousands of people, I am convinced that God is constantly grieved that we have somehow laid hold of the idea that it is tee who have to whip up what we can recognize as *faith*. The same is true of prayer. If your prayer life seems to you to be vapid and only half alive, do you feel guilty about it? That re sponse is also wrong. Wrong for me, too, and yet I still have to remind myself of its wrongness. The same is true of what appears to be our lack of growth, our lack of giving, of praise, and so on.

We are heading in the wrong direction when we expend one single minute in conscientious but useless effort to whip up any of the qualities of the Christian life.

Every characteristic of the "life hid in Christ" men-tioned in this little book, and many more characteristics be-sides, are, by our own efforts, out of reach. Oh, I know how many sermons have been preached on our commitment to God, our lack of faith, our shallow prayer-lives, our pitifully small gifts, our lack of resemblance to Christ, our laziness in service. While waiting for another TV program that I wanted to watch, I listened to the ending of a sermon by a perspiring, thumping, earnest gentleman that, *if* I'd missed the point of this chapter, would have had me crawling under the rug with guilt.

The God of the Cross and the Open Tomb did not come to earth to cover us over with guilt. He came to free us from it, and anyone can be free of the self-struggle in the life with Christ if he or she will face the one, irrevocable fact that *what really matters*–only thing that makes it all possible—is the fact of God's eternal commitment to us.

The Eternal God of the universe, the Creator, the Good Shepherd, the Comforter, the Greatest Teacher, the Savior, is and has always been *totally committed* to you and to me, to everyone who will or who has ever lived on the earth for as long as that God has been in existence. And there has never been a time when God was not in existence.

If for some reason I had to blot out every other word in the entire Bible, I would cling for dear life to these *lifelines* from the first chapter of John's Gospel:

> In the beginning was the Word, and the
> Word was with God, and the Word was God.
> The same was in the beginning with God.
> All things were made by him; and without him
> was not anything made that was made. . .
> And the Word was made flesh, and dwelt
> among us. . . No man hath seen God at
> any time; the only begotten Son . . .
> he hath declared him.

With an amiable nod to those who grow anxious about my commitment because I don't always set down the numbers of every verse and chapter when I use quotations from the Bible, I will tell you that glorious passage is to be found this way: Begin John's Gospel with chapter 1 —read the first three verses, then verse 14, then verse 18. What goes between is marvelous, but these tie together to give me all I really need to believe that the true nature of the God who created us is discoverable in Jesus Christ.

There is no way we can stake our daily or our eternal lives on His commitment to us, unless we *know* beyond the shadow of any doubt that the One who says, "Follow me," is the One who can let the simplest among us know what God is like in His intentions toward us all. "Without him [Jesus, the Word was not anything made that was made." As usual, I have cho- sen the Bang James version here. The literature is too magnificent to miss: "Without him was not anything made that was made." A perfect sentence, but also a giant beam of light on the unalterable fact that the Word, Jesus Christ Him- self, was not only present at Creation, but that He is also the Creator. "The Word was with God and the Word was God."

Again, the italics are mine, but to me every word in the passage quoted above from the Gospel of John could be italicized. It is that important to everything that has to do with everyone God loves, and that is everyone who has ever lived and who will ever live.

In chapter 8 we looked at the importance of knowing Him as He really is. One of my older books. *What Is God Like?*, has to be the most important I've ever written, not because it is so well written, but because it carries the one key to coping with life. I have spent hours leafing back through fifteen or more of my earlier books while thinking my way through this one. The necessity of our having at least some idea of the true nature of God Himself runs through those books like a bright thread. I have looked at tragedy, at monotony, at failure, at disappointment, at death, at grief, at one dark corner of the human dilemma after another, and always the Answer is: This, too, can be coped with if we know God's intentions toward us in it.

But there is no way to know His intentions unless we know Him. I repeat: my commitment to Jesus Christ is permanent—life without Him would for me be one-dimensional—but my commitment is far from flawless. It runs an often erratic course, because a perfectly committed follower would always obey, never disobey, and who does always obey? Certainly not I. A recent example: At a most difficult place in a complex book I was writing, unavoidably I had to stop and spend time with dear people who would never have understood that I was scared and uptight and rebellious in my heart because I had to leave the manuscript. Scared? You bet I was scared. I had worked so hard to reach that place in the book. I had been concerned that I wasn't capable of handling it anyway, and so scared is a mild word. Of course, because I was scared, wrenching myself away made me uptight. And be cause my *own* commitment to Him is flawed, I gave in to quite natural human rebellion. My father always said you could hang your clothes on my line. I do happen to be able to *sound* Christian when I don't *feel* Christian. I can say what's expected of me, and because I've had to make so many public appearances, I can cover my true feelings with quite convinc ing prose. Of course, I don't fool me. And naturally, I don't fool God.

As I dressed to keep this "appointment" I so dreaded, I

said this to the Lord: "All right. You know how scared I am that I'll lose the tiny hold I have just managed to get on that chapter I'm writing. You also know what ugly, demeaning thoughts I'm thinking. You know how uncommitted I'm acting and how soon I 'll be writing another book in which I'll have to say a lot about commitment to You. You know the comer I'm in. You also know that I know perfectly well that if I let go of my rebellions, You will show me how to make this interruption redemptive. Well, I'm not ready to stop rebelling yet. Maybe when I walk up the steps to the restaurant where I'm meeting these insistent people. I'll let go and allow your peace to take over. I don't want to be scared and I don't want to feel rebellious. But I'm scared *and* fighting. Make me willing to let You handle the whole thing—including me before and after I get back to my desk."

That's a prayer? It certainly is. And, of course, He knew how it was going to turn out all along. Briefly, what happened was that, surprisingly to me, one of those present whom I'd never met was not only interesting, but truly *resilient*, and without knowing it, she invited me to remember my commitment. I had been with the other four people often in the past. I knew the whole session would mean the kind of small talk that, at best, makes me fidget. Not so. The new member of the party unconsciously allowed God to remind me of my buried sense of humor about myself. I lost a day's work—I often have to lose a day's work because of some obligation or other—but the next morning the sticky spot in the manuscript on which I was struggling seemed almost to handle itself.

This happened because He took over in spite of me. And why is God able to do these inner things for us? Because He is God, naturally, but also because even when our commit ment to Him falters. His to us is as steady and unshakable as it has been from the beginning. Especially when we are recal citrant—and that usually means we are hurting ourselves in the process—He proves the durability of His eternal commit ment to us.

My memory tells me that while I was writing *The Wider Place*, this amazing truth about His commitment to us lighted up my mind. Since that moment I have stopped struggling to perfect my own commitment to Him. I can't perfect it. If my mail is any indication, hundreds of His sincere followers are still struggling to perfect their commitments. In fact, in some Christian groups they keep committing themselves over and over. We don't need to. I see it as futile. Instead, I have begun to count, even when Fm annoyed, on His commitment to me. I find that by doing so I can begin to put my foolish struggles into perspective far more quickly than if I agonize over my own stubborn streaks.

Where did I find this (to me) rest-giving truth? As I recall, I found it in one of John's letters. In I John 4:19—one of the shortest verses in the Bible:

We love him, because he first loved us.

I have a friend who still enjoys trying out the old smiling trick when she rides to and from work on a Chicago bus. She will focus at the grumpiest-looking face and smile until that person smiles back at her—or turns away entirely. I'm told that mothers smile their babies into smiling back. Well, God loves us into loving Him back—unless we turn away entirely. And to me that means that since He is love, according to die same "beloved disciple," John, His commitment in love to us has been forever. If everyone who has ever loved God was *loved into it*, how can such commitment be questioned?

"Don't tell me God loves me. If He did. He'd never have taken my son's life in that car accident."

Where in the Bible are we told that God will, while we're on this earth, eliminate accidents? Again, Jesus reminded us that "in this world ye shall have tribulation." But He added: "Be of good cheer. I have overcome the world."

Isn't that lady's son still dead from the accident? Yes. But who first got hold of the notion that the God of the Cross, who left the Father's side to get into the earthly mess with us, would so weaken us as to make us cosmic pets simply because we have begun to follow Him?

We dare not question His commitment to us because one ghastly, rainy night the driver of the truck that crashed into this woman's son had been drinking too much. Jesus does not stop sin in the world. He offers redemption from it. And to me that redemption will always include the suffering that results from sin, or even from an unavoidable accident. He will, if we give Him a chance, redeem the unmerited suffering, too.

Where is His commitment to us in suffering? To those who knew His love before the sorrow struck, He is immediately found to be there. He has been there all the time, so the quick, desperate turn to Him will reveal His presence. In the hours of weeping He is there. When we feel most alone, when the pain and heartbreak are so thick around us so that we feel far from God, He is never far from us. "Jesus wept," we are told, when He learned that His earthly friend Lazarus had died. Didn't He know that He Himself would soon raise Lazarus from the grave? Yes, He knew that. I believe Jesus wept for the pain of Mary and Martha, the grieving sisters.

My brother, Joe, has been directly in His Presence now

for more than two months as I write this. The Lord God isn't weeping over Joe, but He does weep with Millie, Joe's heart broken wife, as she makes her way—some days fairly well, others in near desperation—through the first weeks and months alone. For half my own life I didn't know of God's commitment to us. I'm grateful every day that Millie does know. Her enormous loss is not diminished, but God's commitment to her in her grief does not waver. His commitment to you in your grief does not—will never— waver. We all have His word for it. Jesus Himself, knowing us as only He does, made this very, very plain:

> . . . lo, I am with you alway,
> even unto the end of the world.

He spoke those words of commitment to His grieving disci ples just before He left them to return to the Father. The more I think about what He said the more clearly I realize that *He had no choice* but to say that He would never, never really leave them. That He, the Master they loved and fol lowed, would be with them always. Only He knew them well enough to realize that nothing less than His Presence with them, in a way that would be still closer than before, could give them the courage to go on without the actual sight and touch of Him. Nothing less than *being with us* helps, and so He has worked out a way to be "closer than breathing, nearer than hands and feet." When we speak of His Spirit with us now to someone who does not know of friendship with Him, we are considered peculiar. The most natural phenomenon of all to the Christian is that God did work out a way to be with us now.

His commitment to us had no beginning, as He Himself

had none. He is the beginning. And He is the end. "I am Alpha and Omega, the beginning and the end." "Lo, I am with you alway. . . " A commitment of that nature can be counted on, and we can count on it because God cannot change.

"God has turned away from me," an elderly man wrote not long ago from a nursing home.

Answering his letter was not easy. I can certainly understand why an ailing, aging person, deserted by his children as this man was, unable to die although he longed to, could think that the God of love had turned away from him. I told him that I tried, at least, to understand. But I also felt I had to tell him that if God had indeed turned away. He had also lied to us all. In the Old Testament and in the New, we can hear Him say:

> Be strong and of good courage,
> fear not, nor be afraid of them:
> for the Lord thy God,
> he it is that doth go with thee;
> he will not fail thee,
> nor forsake thee.

That is Deuteronomy 31:6. I put down my eternal weight on these two commitments of God from the New Test- ament: "Lo, I am with you alway. . ." and "I will never leave you nor forsake you."

"I will never leave you nor forsake you." That's so simple and plain that it can, at least in time, penetrate grief and desolation. I mentioned that I am writing to a young woman on death row. Hers must sometimes be the kind of desolation which only God can penetrate. He does. Most of the time she is certain that she is not the only occupant of that cell: He has not forsaken her.

The assurances of His commitment are nearly as endless as the commitment itself. Another one that never fails to rest me is one I have no trouble understanding.

He is the author and finisher of our faith.

As I said earlier, I can understand about authors. The same person who begins a book is there at the finish, as I am here now. There was a day when I began chapter i, and today I will finish. Once more I will know the elevation of being able to write in my date book: The End. The same author—the same person—has been at this typewriter day in and day out until this final day.

The same Person has been committed to you from the beginning and the same Person with the same steady commitment to you will be there at the end and beyond. Jesus said that He would be with us—'even unto the end of the world." He will be. He is like that. Why didn't He include beyond the end of the world? Because then we will need no reminders of His constancy. It is while we are still here in earth's school, learning how to be at home with Him, that we need the reminders. Beyond the end of the world, beyond these daily hassles and joys and interruptions and delights, we will be with Him in such a way that no one could forget what He's really like.

For now, count on His commitment to you and watch all else begin to fall into place. Watch faith and prayer and praise and giving and service and your commitment—every thing begin to *happen* as a result of paying attention to the all-important fact of His commitment to you. To me.

We are His responsibility—all the way from Creation through Redemption and into His Presence. In Him we are complete. In Him we can be "content with such things as we have" or do not have. Because He has said that He would never leave us nor forsake us.

"Jesus Christ, the same yesterday, today, and forever." No circumstance, no person, can change Him. He is. He is with us *always*. And He is eternally committed to you and to me.

Everything we need or long for is contained in His ever lasting commitment to us. That, now and in the end, is *what really matters*.